TALES OF TOGO

TOGO

A YOUNG WOMAN'S SEARCH FOR HOME IN WEST AFRICA

Meredith Pike-Baky

A PEACE CORPS WRITERS BOOK

TALES OF TOGO: A Young Woman's Search for Home in West Africa
A Peace Corps Writers Book—an Imprint of Peace Corps Worldwide

Printed in the United States of America
by Peace Corps Writers of Oakland, California.

For more information, contact peacecorpsworldwide@gmail.com.
Peace Corps Writers and the Peace Corps Writers colophon
are trademarks of PeaceCorpsWorldwise.org.

ISBN-13: 978-1-950444-13-7
Library of Congress Control Number: 2020910161

First Peace Corps Writers Edition, September 2020

Dedicated to the women of Togo

whose granddaughters, daughters, sisters and mothers

taught me the value of openness, hard work,

resilience, cooperation and joy.

Learning from them was an early step in the search for home.

And to the memory of Mark Ali,

colleague, teacher, writer and friend.

The Bight of Benin is a bay on the western coast of Africa...It is known for its dangerous undertow...I first ventured into the Bight of Benin more than thirty-five years ago, and I have never really left.

—**KELLY J. MORRIS,** *The Bight of Benin: Short Fiction*

West African *Adinkra* symbols are visible everywhere in the region, printed on fabric, carved into wood, painted on buildings or busses or advertising boards. They reflect wisdom passed down from generations. This symbol can be translated to "I change or transform my life."

CONTENTS

CONTINENT OF AFRICA

TOGO

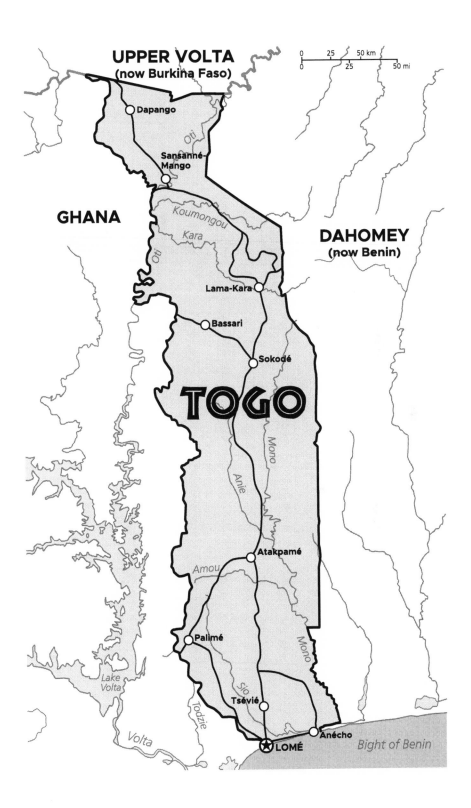

Painting on a school notebook cover by Nathaniel, Togolese artist and
street vendor

[When] I went to the small country of Togo, in West Africa, to work on a girls' education project...I went in search of myself...What I found instead was a fascinating West African web of gender, cultural, and romantic complexity...

—**LAURIE L. CHARLES**, *Intimate Colonialism:*
Head, Heart & Body in West African Development Work

PREFACE

TO LOOK AT PHOTOS, peruse my vast slide collection, read my journals, or follow my mother's updates in annual holiday rhymes, you might presume that my emergence into adulthood was ordinary. I was an ambitious student surrounded by many friends and engaged in productive activities. I studied Spanish in addition to French, joined the International Club, and made friends with exchange students from Norway and Finland, an early sign that distant and unknown places lured me. I was curious about the world. The enchantment of life beyond my home and family fed a hunger for freedom and adventure. I was eager to strike out and create a life I could steer.

But the truth is, life hadn't always been easy. Early photographs of our sunny smiling family surely didn't reveal some rather non-ordinary details. The pictures conceal my mother's episodic drinking problem. They belie my father's swift and silent abandonment of us, his hasty marriage to a family friend and his continuing distance, though he lived four blocks away. I yearned for a home with less confusion and unpredictability in relationships.

I wasn't at all confused about my role as citizen of the world. People across continents, countries, ethnic groups, economic classes and political loyalties had to come together, to see each other's perspectives and opt, always, for compromise and mutual respect. Going to college in Berkeley in the 70's strengthened this conviction. As a feisty and fashion-averse undergraduate sporting unfettered long hair, jeans and a sweatshirt, I believed that people were born to help each other, that the stranger on the sidewalk who dropped his bag of groceries or tripped on the curb deserved my assistance. Conversely, I trusted that my compassionate landlady would accept my rent check one day late. Good people broke rules to help each other out. I was idealistic about how young activists could improve not just international relations, but generational discord, even though I hadn't been terribly successful in convincing my ex-military father about our government's inappropriate actions in Vietnam.

Though I sought adventure and was intrigued by people who held romantic, exotic beliefs, who spoke other languages and lived far away, my experience was limited. I hadn't traveled internationally and my knowledge of foreign lands was limited to the Canadian maple leaf charm on my silver bracelet, my 7th grade fictional account of bikeriding through Sweden, my stamp collection and reading. I'd read about a love affair across castes in India and had closely followed my childhood friend's travels in Australia. Most of the required reading I'd done as an English major, the work of British poets, Shakespeare, and James Joyce, had provided little insight into contemporary cultures or issues. There were no assignments about the war in Vietnam, racism, civil rights. However, many of us believed that international travel supplemented school learning and that relationships with people from other cultures would fill the gaps of a traditional education.

Peace Corps was a vehicle to relevant learning, cultural exchange and meaningful work. I reasoned that moving abroad under the guidance of a government agency that campaigned for global understanding would be easier and safer than setting out on my own. If I managed to be accepted, I could travel, get professional training, meet people from far away and escape the disappointing relationships at home.

When I was accepted, it felt as if my real life began. I moved across the world from northern California to Togo, West Africa, after a stop for training in Canada. I made close friends with people I had previously judged to be square, straight, dull. I experienced unimaginable generosity on the part of children willing to do what I always needed and never requested, and especially from my high school students who forgave rookie teaching and thinly veiled political opinions. A thwarted sweetheart swiftly bailed me out of a medical crisis. I worked hard to feel at home and to understand what home was. Was home a place? a family? a feeling? I was ready to find out far, far away.

In spite of guidance, many regulations and rigid rules, I was mostly left alone to commit my own blunders, to veer off course, to lose my way. I stumbled through mishaps and cheered myself forward through small victories. The experiences and relationships taught me what home and family could be. They changed me in ways I could not have predicted, taught me lessons I didn't seek, and resulted in a lifelong attachment to Africa. The tales that follow are my attempt to unravel the origins of such a fierce loyalty. I emerged aware of a much grander world and of the many ways I could become a creative and productive citizen within it.

Togo, one of the tiniest countries on the continent, opened a door to Africa, but it was hardly representative of all African life and cultures. My lens was tiny, like Togo, wholly personal and fraught with the preoccupations of transitioning from adolescent to adult in the 1970's, a historically dramatic time. I arrived in Togo eager to escape the disarray of family relationships and the political turmoil at home, to learn to teach and to travel. Togo, too, was in the beginning stages of delayed independence, having declared an end to French rule a decade earlier. Now, happily, both Togo and I were on the threshold of a new era, a heady, hopeful time for both of us: newly independent African nation and volunteer-visitor-emerging young adult.

Now, so many years later, I think back to how my experiences as a Peace Corps volunteer in Togo shaped who I am today and determined how I've lived my life, personally and professionally. How extraordinary it is to realize that a mere two years could plant the seeds for the following 50, 60, even 70 years!

My Togolese friends taught me the magic of storytelling in order to teach, to learn, to share. The tales in this collection are like the beads of a necklace, *les perles d'un collier*, whole in themselves, and at the same time integral parts of a longer story when threaded on a string. Each is introduced by a nod to another writer of Africa, emulating the widespread practice of having friends gather and honoring ancestors by tipping cups of local brew onto the ground. Symbolically or literally, the gesture signals gratitude, obligation, continuity. I have attempted the same practice in the epigraphs for each chapter. As a new teacher, I became a learner over and over again. Lessons layered upon experiences formed the bedrock for the many years that followed, and continue to breathe life into the person I am today. Come, partake, enjoy.

FRESH VISTAS:
LOOKING OUT AND AHEAD

STOOD ON A GRASSY HILLSIDE looking down across long flat fields that stretched to the river's edge. The water was glistening, reflecting the light of the setting sun in shifting patterns. Lush green was directly below me; silver and muted lavender formed a backdrop from the mountains beyond. It was the end of a day full of people and classes, brain-busting French language lessons and cultural "do's" and "don'ts".

Sing-along with Togo trainees in La Pocatière, Canada

Don't offer anything with your left hand. Tip a sip to the ancestors. Always ask about people's families. Never overlook greetings. I listed the guidelines I'd been learning.

"*Ouf!*" I blurted, an expression of happy exhaustion, pursing my lips and sending out a blast of breath. Now, alone, on a northern Quebec hilltop, I laughed at myself trying so hard to sound native. I was away from the noise and activity of our back-to-back training sessions, by myself on this hilltop now. We'd spent all day scurrying from lessons in French to English-teaching to African cultural imperatives. *Such busy-ness, such life direction, and here, such beauty.*

In the early 1970's I was in my early 20's, living for the moment in northern Quebec, Canada. I was at the beginning of a two-month orientation in this Francophone (French-speaking) province. This was the first stage of training to become a Peace Corps Volunteer. Fifty trainers, twenty of them African, were also here to teach about a hundred trainees what we needed to know before setting foot in one of nine West African countries. We would be sent to teach English in Cameroun, Congo, Côte d'Ivoire, Dahomey, Haute-Volta, Niger, Senegal, Tchad and Togo. We Peace Corps trainees were a diverse group from many different parts of the U.S., two-thirds of us women in our twenties, three with husbands, four *stagiares* (trainees) forty and older, and about a dozen African-Americans, all of us eager to learn. Our lodging was a boarding school that looked like a medieval castle. The small town a block away boasted three bars and two general stores. Behind the school the St. Lawrence River tugged its shiny magnificence from east to west. I was transported by the beautiful surroundings, the quaint village, the friends that I was making each day, and my slowly growing ability to communicate in

French. All was a swirl of learning. The pace, the learning, the rigor. I clenched my fists and held my body still to keep from jumping up and down and darting here and there with delight.

Now alone in the afternoon light, overlooking the river, I practiced what we'd learned in French class earlier, connecting words so tightly that they ran into each other and sped past silent consonants. *Je-n'ai-pas-écrit-à-ma-famille-aujourd'hui,* confessing that I hadn't written home yet that day. I recited a sentence with direct and indirect objects from the morning's lesson, trying to make it sound effortless. *Il me l'a donné hier.* Eel-muh-lah-DUNnay-ee-air. It was slowly getting easier to insert the end of a sentence between the subject and auxiliary verb, but boy, did it require supreme concentration. *L'as-tu lui déjà donné?* LAH-too-louie-day-jah-DUNNAY?

I was easily distracted thinking of the dancing the night before. We Americans were "studying" dance too, in this linguistic and cultural immersion program. I snickered at how we were trying to move our bodies to the rhythms, imitating our African guides.

"*Comme ça!*" a willowy Senegalese French teacher demonstrated effortless torso and hip isolation in time to the music. He made it look so easy. Most of us couldn't even catch the rhythm in our feet, much less our torsos. *Argh! It was so tough!*

Everything was challenging: the acrobatics French required of my mouth and the coordinated stepping and swiveling of African dance moves. So much was so new. Then, when I was feeling most daunted, a soft breeze came up the bluff and I refocused on this magical place and was uplifted. It really didn't matter how fast I learned French or how well I danced; everything was enchanting.

"Eh! Mademoiselle! Ça va aujourd'hui?!" I spotted my young friend Denis calling to me as he clambered up the grassy hillside. If my French comprehension had improved at all, twelve-year-old Denis deserved most of the credit. We'd met one afternoon when I was sitting out a volleyball game, having injured my back from a spectacular spike the day before, securing a victory for my team but preventing me from future play. Denis had walked up from the village to watch the game; he was squatting in shorts on the slope beside the field, hugging bare bony knees.

"Pourquoi vous ne jouez pas, Mademoiselle?" he asked with big curious eyes, encouraging me to get back in the game. I explained that my injured back was keeping me sidelined. *"Et alors!"* Well then, he retorted. He jumped to his feet and cheerfully proposed that we spend afternoons together so that he could show me around the village. I thought it would be a great way to practice my French.

"En français, n'est-ce pas?" I asked, both of us agreeing through laughter. I was so cheered up by being able to practice my French and explore the village that frustration with my injury nearly disappeared. So Denis and I'd begun meeting most afternoons. He took me to places I hadn't seen, the whole time speaking in a twangy dialect I was beginning to understand.

"Whey Deneese! Ça va byeh!" I tried to imitate his pronunciation as I called back to him on that afternoon.

"Fait beau aujourd'hui, n'est-ce pas?" He shouted, words all jumbled in the front of his mouth. Denis' huge blue eyes and long skinny limbs reminded me of a cartoon character. He'd ushered in such a fun, light-

hearted element to my life during the intense training, one day presenting me proudly to a couple of his 10-year-old friends, and on another day explaining a quirky French expression with great patience. To show my gratitude, I was teaching Denis to whistle with four fingers. He'd stick two fingers from each hand into opposite sides of his mouth and wait for instructions.

"Et voila, Denis!" There ya go, I'd say, but his permanent smile made it challenging and the whistle never materialized. Always so cheerful, he laughed often at my frequent misunderstandings and the words I couldn't understand through his accent. I got bolder speaking to him, trying new expressions and mimicking his. Our conversations accompanied us to the local cemetery, around the small *potagers*, vegetable gardens beside each small house in the village, to the long fields beside the river, to the many religious statues and to this hilltop. As he approached me running in long strides that afternoon, he caught his breath and apologized. He didn't have time to take me anywhere that day, but he'd see me the next afternoon.

"Ah demaah! See you tomorrow!" he called, reversing his direction and loping down the hill, his curly brown hair blowing as he waved and disappeared. I pulled at the lanyard attached to the zipper on my windbreaker, a hand-crafted gift he'd made especially for me. I shivered with pleasure in the cooling afternoon breeze.

There I was, zigging and zagging across the world, geographically and emotionally. I'd just left my home in California to become a teacher in

West Africa by way of Canada. Oh yes, I'd left home before. I'd crossed the country to attend my first two years of college and travelled with friends to what I'd considered distant places like Oregon, Florida, and Washington DC. These destinations once seemed remote. Africa was going to be new, exotic, and really far away. Already Quebec seemed so very different and I was only at the first step of a much longer journey.

My friendship with Denis had helped me bridge differences between the familiar and all that was new. I was forging new relationships with my family members too as we'd begun a lively exchange of letters. My younger sister wrote a sentimental farewell card, surprising me with her concern for my safety. I was warmed by her anxiety. My father, normally silent, and my stepmother, preoccupied with her own life, had become unexpectedly attentive since I'd left. Dad, always taciturn and usually too busy for me, sent a letter that began, "It is most satisfying to parents when their small fry finds a goal and a purpose that she believes in, is willing to work hard to accomplish it, and has the ambition and confidence for real achievement..." I brushed aside his formality, happy to learn of his interest in my life. My stepmom sent Draft #1 of her shopping list. "Buy me lots of fabric and look for wooden sculptures— you know how I love masks!" The unusual attention buoyed me up. My recent boyfriend surprised me too with his letters and calls. I didn't understand why he was calling me every night and wrote about it in my journal. He seemed to be much more attentive than when I'd been at home. My childhood girlfriends offered to write lots of letters, send me extra underwear and check in with my mom, as they were privy to my concerns about her drinking and general well-being. And my mom, who always championed me even at her worst times, responded promptly to my frequent requests. Her chirpy letters arrived every other day alongside small packages. I received batteries, a pair of Keds, rubber sandals, sheet music and family photos. "I'm so excited for you! You'll do great! I already miss you so much! I'll share your letters with my students!" My new life had become hers too, and her enthusiasm was promising.

I peered out at the long green *Quebecois* fields below me and thought again about how the last few years in Berkeley had set me up for adventure with an attitude. As a UC student during the Free Speech Movement and the campaigns for feminism, Civil Rights—and most explosive—protests against continuing military aggression in Vietnam, I'd been offered an alternative college course schedule. Music 27B was supplanted by anti-war silk-screening. Instead of studying Mahler symphonies, my music classmates and I had produced bright, artful posters displaying slogans that became code words and chants for the era. Colorful banners displaying slogans like "Stop the War" and "Peace is Patriotic" hung from windows all over campus. As I made my way to class, I sidestepped National Guard soldiers. Taping my windows shut to prevent tear gas from seeping in during almost daily confrontations between students and soldiers, I listened to daily drum circles from the street corner below, as motley groups of antiwar protesters pounded out rhythms of harmony and solidarity. I marched, attended sit-ins, read Gloria Steinem and Eldridge Cleaver, and decried "The Establishment." I'd learned all the words to all the songs in the musical *Hair*. I boycotted Bank of America for its ties to apartheid South Africa. Berkeley introduced me to the power and contagious excitement of peaceful protest and gradually we saw our activism make a difference. Campus rules relaxed, more politicians questioned our role in Southeast Asia, and increasing numbers of young men sought clever ways to avoid the draft.

The idealism I'd cultivated in Berkeley made me a perfect candidate for the Peace Corps. John F. Kennedy's initial call to "do for your country" was an inspiring nudge to continue my activism. Through the Peace Corps I could work at an important job and escape from the confusion of home. I'd get training, learn professional skills, travel, receive healthcare, be able to tuck away money each month to pay back college debts, and have a small savings for my return after two years of service.

Unfortunately, there was a long list of requirements to apply to be a volunteer and no guarantee of getting accepted. With hundreds more applicants than positions, I tried to be patient through the interminable decision-making period. I pinned my hopes and my qualifications on a good attitude, tutoring done in a poor community during college, my political biases and my current boyfriend, a grad student from Ghana. I was feeling desperate to move on with my life, feeling trapped by college loans and recovering from a premature marriage.

I waited to hear from Peace Corps and cleverly protected myself from the possibility of not getting accepted by dreaming up an alternate route: life among the scenic golden hills of northern California. I could become a lifeguard. My father, president of the homeowners' association at a high-end residential development in the Sierra foothills, had benevolently reserved a role for me. I imagined wistfully that it would be nice to live near my dad—maybe we'd even develop a relationship.

Finally, when I had nearly lost hope, a packet arrived in the mail. "It's from the Peace Corps and it's fat!" my mom called out.

"This invitation is for one of eight Francophone countries," the letter stated. "The most sought-after prize among young Africans today is an education. When Peace Corps came to Francophone Africa in 1962, governments turned to the new American organization to provide badly-needed teachers of English." I jumped up and down, clutched the letter to my chest, waved it in the air and hugged my mom.

"Woohoo!"

"Hot diggedy!" my mom exclaimed.

My father and stepmom made plans to visit me wherever I was assigned, my sister worried about the unknowns. After securing Conscientious Objector status, my brother set off on his own journey around the world, offering a supportive form of parallel travel. At the threshold of being further apart than we'd ever been, my family came together. I figured that this was what it felt like to be close to your family.

My friends claimed they could never go away for two whole years. "One year, maybe, but never TWO!" So different from them, I was only delighted, giddy at all that I'd be pushed to do, the surprises I'd encounter, the people I'd meet, the changes I'd experience. For me, the long time away, the at-best intermittent communication with friends and family, no telephone access, unpredictable mail service and simple, basic living conditions seemed thrilling. I wanted to be President John F. Kennedy's solution, the world's hope for the future, a broker for international understanding. "Life in the Peace Corps will not be easy," Kennedy warned new volunteers. I was ready!

During the weeks in northern Quebec, I was learning about West Africa. I read excerpts from Chinua Achebe's *Things Fall Apart* and Camara Laye's *L'Enfant Noir*. Evening lectures on family life taught us that cousins and close friends in African cultures were considered brothers and sisters and that every child belonged to every adult. We enjoyed a celebratory meal of bar-b-qued goat and rice. I pored over a map of the continent, particularly the northern part, with its vast desert, its many crooked country borders, the concentration of cities along the coast, and their unfamiliar names. Below the Sahara, national borders got complicated. It was easier to remember the names of countries when I associated them with my friends' assignments or trainers' native countries. Evelyn was going to la Côte d'Ivoire, Ivory Coast. Our dance teacher Boubacar was from Senegal. Gaston, my very favorite trainer, was from Niger and Marcus, another volunteer, was going to Chad. I learned that I was being sent to Togo, a sliver of a country. I knew it was small, with fewer westerners than Ivory Coast or Senegal. That was my preference. It was also next to Ghana, where my friend Isaac was from. If I got really lonely or confused, I could skip across the border and visit Isaac's family.

"Brrrr!" I rubbed my arms as the northern sun dropped beyond green fields and the temperature cooled. I anticipated what was to come. Turning away from the river and quickening my pace, I began my walk back to the school to return before dark. I looked forward to dancing after dinner, hopeful that my moves and the lilting rhythms of the music were becoming better synchronized. I was speaking more French and receiving encouraging letters from my family. I inhaled the cool air of dusk as fresh vistas in all parts of my life came into view.

In the first days here, with the heat, the food, intestinal troubles, and the sense of having been pulled up by the roots, I seemed to lose about 20 percent of my energy...the rigid schedule and the long confinement with others rattled our nerves.

—**GEORGE PACKER**, *The Village of Waiting*

AFRICA SHOCK

TOGO SITS SNUGLY on West Africa's Gold Coast, tucked in between Ghana and Dahomey (renamed Bénin in 1990). Togo, roughly the size of West Virginia but surely not its shape, stretches long and lean, from the coast of the Gulf of Bénin, with its lush red-earthed southern region, to the dry dusty savannah in the north, which borders land-locked La Haute Volta, Upper Volta, (Burkina Faso today). Name changes to several African countries in the last fifty years reflect efforts

With Sundia and Jean, a friend, on day of departure from Lomé

to shed colonial labels and hint at the randomness of country borders, particularly along the Gold Coast. Locals in this region originally settled horizontally, along broad latitudes extending from what is now Liberia to Nigeria. Traders forging lucrative routes, explorers seeking potential wealth and colonialists racing for land changed settlement patterns. In the early part of the twentieth century, lines of unity and traditional authority were blocked and redrawn by European powers appropriating Africa for their own interests. They established country divisions without respect to ethnic groups or family lines, often placing brothers and sisters across national borders. In order to understand how West Africa was organized, I imagined chopping a serpentine Bûche de Noël into irregular slices, then disconnecting and repositioning the swirls so that they seemed unrelated.

During our training in Canada, we were given brief history lessons. Volunteers in my Togo-bound group got a quick overview of the country's history and geography. We learned about the country's four regions extending from south to north (Maritime, Plateaux, Centrale, Savanes), its twenty-seven dialects and more than thirty ethnic groups. Today the region of Kara constitutes a fifth region. All of this information, so many languages and so many cultures, was abstract until I arrived in the country and set out to talk to people and move around. It seemed everyone spoke a different language. Those who came from the north looked different than those from the south. I was grateful to have Peace Corps—the staff and our orientation sessions—help me make sense of the material I hadn't really internalized earlier. Studying facts was a far cry from on-the-ground understanding of those facts.

When we first arrived in the capital city of Lomé, after an endless series of stops and short flights along the West African coast, where we delivered fellow volunteers to their assigned countries, we were introduced to Edith. Edith was American and the manager of an inn where we would be living for the month-long "in-country" training. It may have been sheer exhaustion from the long trip from North America or the sadness at saying goodbye to so many new friends at the conclusion of our time in Quebec. Or it may have been anxiety about where I would be placed, if I would like it, if I could manage all that was required. Most likely, it was the disappointment at discovering that Edith was not Togolese, but American. I thought for sure she was African. Dark and smooth-skinned, so sure of herself, she moved steadily with easy confidence. There was no hint of a smile in her focused gaze.

"H-e-e-y-y-y. Como talley vooo?" Her accent, so non-native, gave it away instantly. I shuddered in embarrassment and regretted her lack of authenticity. Yet her straight-ahead no-nonsense style suggested that she wasn't at all uncomfortable as a foreigner and as a struggling French speaker. I studied her, waited for a smile, some suggestion that she was kind, supportive, maybe understanding.

"Hurry up! Sit down! Move over there!" Her commands felt like reprimands. We'd just arrived, were weary, confused, befuddled by this new living situation. Edith scared me.

"Take your affairs to your rooms now and come back for dinner in ten minutes. Do you hear? TEN MINUTES! If you're late, no meal. And whatever you do, DON'T ask to change roommates!"

I soon learned that Edith (Ay-deet in French) had arrived in Lomé shortly before the rest of us, repatriating to West Africa from Chicago. Actually, she'd landed in English-speaking Ghana, the country directly west of Togo, just when that country had met sudden economic decline. Noting that in nearby Togo, there was plenty to drink, much to see, but nowhere to stay, she established a rest stop for travelers, proving to herself and announcing frequently to everyone around her that she had landed in just the right place at the right time. First, Peace Corps learned of her nursing background and enlisted her as Medical Officer. Next, Peace Corps chose her inn as the headquarters for our group's in-country training.

"Providential!" she exclaimed to us. "It was meant to be!" I wasn't so sure.

Edith equipped her inn with bunk beds made of freshly chopped sweet-smelling African teak. She developed a menu of sound-alike American dishes though they held little resemblance to the familiar.

"I can't swallow," I overheard someone whisper as we struggled to eat peanut butter sandwiches. I saw others wince when we downed glasses of unimaginably sour "fresh orange juice." Edith didn't bother with our early resistance. She must have anticipated it.

"Try this!" she offered.

"Oh, the stuff in the dish is a local version of ketchup."

"You'll be fine with the heat."

"No need to complain. You'll get used to it!"

She played The Expert on Everything to other residents and passers-by, but mostly to us, unsettled and bewildered volunteers. To me she seemed to think we'd been coddled in Quebec and were spoiled, entitled

young Americans. I wished she were Togolese. Then I could have forgiven her lack of empathy. Peace Corps capitalized on Edith's ingenuity,
relieved to have a local venue to host training programs. As more travelers discovered the inn, she expanded into the bicycle repair shop next
door and introduced new menu options. *Doyenne* of her hotel, *chef* at her
restaurant, and *Directrice-Infirmière* of what also became a pop-up clinic,
Edith's Inn was an American oasis.

But the inn was no oasis for me. I rarely talked to the various visitors, preferring to read on my bunk, review handouts from our Canadian
training in La Pocatière, or write letters. This didn't feel like Africa. I
didn't really like these people. I hadn't come to Lomé to meet Americans.
Daily doses of English were displeasing. I yearned for the 24-hour French
immersion rule that governed us in Canada. How could I delight in
undersized, overcooked hamburgers? I wanted to eat African food with
my fingers! I wanted to learn the local dialect! I wanted to get away from
America, not seek refuge in it. And in spite of the many warnings, the
lack of hot or drinkable water worried me and made me feel vulnerable
to disease.

My rebellious spirit, my politics, my desire not to be lumped in a
group of young naïve Americans found me irritable. My country's youth
had just emerged from a turbulent Civil Rights Movement and we'd
been emboldened by having successfully demanded an end to the war
in Vietnam. I wanted to stay loyal to these historic struggles and disas-
sociate myself from mainstream America. I was convinced I could do
this even working for a government agency as a Peace Corps Volunteer.
But just to be sure, I requested a post far from the capital and planned
to spend time only with Africans. I'd get so good at French and the local

languages that people wouldn't know I was American. English, Dutch, German—anything was better than being American.

I kept my resentment private, for I was to be at Edith's Inn for only a little over a month. I'd complete my practice teaching, learn a few phrases in local languages and prepare for a permanent assignment in a town hopefully far to the north. "This will be over soon," I muttered several times a day. How different Lomé was from my young friend Denis' Canadian village of La Pocatière. In "La Poc" the days had been too short; in Lomé, they were too long.

Edith rattled on.

"You'll get used to it!"

"It'll be fine!"

"Just take it easy."

How dare Edith think she had something to teach me? She didn't even speak French!

Lomé was shocking. It stank. Men peed in open gutters and spit in the streets. Crowds gathered everywhere. People shouted, cars sped, drivers honked their horns day and night. Kids attacked us, screaming rhythmic demands for money and candy. People blared music from hidden corners. Grown-ups wore pajamas in the daytime. It was miserably humid. I couldn't find my way around. It was dirty and dusty and grim. Where was I? This was nothing like the neat and orderly community we'd left behind in Canada. Where was Denis? Where were our African trainers who'd made everything seem so easy? This was NOT what I expected. I was having frightful dreams, awakening to fears of sudden blindness or yearning for home. This place was wretched.

I shared a small room with two other women and though we found ourselves in impossibly tight quarters—crowded onto bunk beds between large suitcases and boxes of books—what most pushed us up against the other was the unspoken terror we felt at being in such a foreign place. This too fueled my resentment. Aha, I thought. This was why Edith warned us against requesting new roommates. She'd known we'd be uncomfortable. The extensive training program I'd completed, the numerous "cultural immersion" meetings I'd attended, even the relationships I'd forged with my West African mentors had not prepared me for the shock of those first days in Africa.

"*Bonzhuire*" was Edith's afternoon greeting, straddling day and night with her French accent, part Chicago and part southern USA. At least Edith made an effort to speak French, I said to myself, trying my best to be magnanimous, noting that French continued to mystify all of us by its time, gender, and status demands. But I was puzzled by much more than the language. Now in Togo, I couldn't figure out why we'd spent nearly six weeks in northern Quebec preparing for the Gold Coast of West Africa. Why Canada? Had we learned anything of relevance? The glimmering pastel sunsets over the St. Lawrence River, for example, were a harsh contrast to sundown in Lomé. Now in Africa we watched a bright orange equatorial fireball descend in sudden silence. And those polite and curious Québequois children, Denis most notably, who'd met me in the afternoons and had taken me all around town, teaching me to speak French with a twang. How different he was from the ubiquitous throngs of Togolese youth who surrounded us everywhere, open palms thrust forward for treats or money, chanting "*Yovo-Yovo-bon-soir! Ca-va-bien? Merci!*" The melodic polite greeting surely didn't feel friendly: "White man, white man, hello to you! How you doin'? Thank you!"

It was all too much and too different. There'd been the orderly, structured days of training in Quebec in contrast to the chaotic, noisy, throbbing life of Lomé. The clean air, neat gardens, formal people of Quebec vs. the dust, the ditches, and in-your-face gawkers of Togo. Could this really be the first month of two years?! I did what I could to trick myself into feeling comfortable, toggling between yearning for the familiar and seeking the exotic, the new, the different. From my upper bunk, I privately declared my new Sony tape recorder my best friend. I experienced soul connections with Carole King as she mourned, "You're so f-a-a-a-a-r away" and I crooned alongside James Taylor as we went together in our minds to Carolina. I learned every single word of every single song and wrote letters home—two or three a day—decorating them with ornate colored-pencil or marker designs, just so letter-writing would take more time. I longed to feel more in control. Coloring gave me time to imagine somewhere else. I dreamed about my favorite trainer in Quebec, my dearest African friend during training. I imagined the life we'd live together once he completed his studies and returned to his country. He'd explain to his sympathetic parents that he was soon to leave them and his vast collection of siblings and cousins in West Africa to join me, his young American heartthrob who could sing Carole King's complete repertoire. In the evenings, I couldn't sleep and most days, I couldn't eat. I felt nervous, on edge, impatient. Confessing to myself that this idea to come to Africa had been one serious mistake, I admitted that I really should have taken that lifeguard position in California.

My resentment was aimed in all directions. Our Training Director was arrogant. He asked questions like, "Why would a teacher encourage silence from students?" He smacked his lips with the satisfaction that he'd stumped us yet again. My co-trainees were embarrassingly unworldly. How did they not know that La Haute Volta was the country directly north of Togo? Why were they always getting sick? And why was Edith regularly checking in with me, offering something new to eat? How could she help me transition when her pathetic attempts at French showed how she hadn't transitioned herself? Her self-assuredness, her easy living in Lomé, her utter lack of self-consciousness annoyed me the most. "This is just the beginning. You'll get used to things. Don't worry!" She continued her attempts to be positive and encouraging. I felt dangerously close to not wanting things to get better just to prove her wrong. I was a wreck.

"Here, dear," she offered, trying to interest me in a plate of canned sausages. She jabbed a toothpick into the middle of one and thrust it towards me.

"No thanks, Edith, I don't normally eat canned sausages," I tried to be polite.

"You're so picky!" she exclaimed, moving on to Phil, a blond southern California surfer, always relaxed and cheerful. He accepted everything she offered. Reaching up from his seat, he took my sausage.

I charted out my feelings on undersized French binder paper with lines that were spaced too close together for even the tiniest handwriting. "Oppressive," I wrote, reacting to the demands of my new setting. I listed three reasons to stay in Togo (my Dad's expectations, earning money, avoiding embarrassment) and one reason to return home (everything's familiar).

In spite of my misery, the thought of deciding to go home two years early was untenable. Returning to the same people who'd cast aside their early reservations and had come to celebrate my decision to move to

Africa was simply *insupportable*. How could I face my mother and my father? What about my stepmother with her heartfelt encouragement and her wacky wish list? And my boyfriend, the Peace Corps recruiter from Ghana who'd worked so hard to get me to Togo in the first place? My best friend at home who'd reluctantly agreed to take my dog? No, there were too many expectations to meet, my career to launch, the world to see. And what about my commitment to President Kennedy's call a decade earlier to be "part of the solution?" I struggled with the extreme discomfort, the unfamiliar tastes and smells, the nervousness and the fear that settled in the pit of my stomach. Yet even when culture shock was at its most intense, when I was weak and skinny and scared, when I couldn't go outside because the stench of urine made my eyes sting and I couldn't languish a moment longer in my room because it was too hot or cluttered with papers or musty and dreadfully oppressive, I realized that I'd have to stay. After two weeks of this, the lack of equilibrium, the knot in my gut, the bad taste in my mouth, an endless headache and terrible longing, something clicked, or broke or snapped. I took charge and bought a cat.

I named the kitten Sundia, short for Sundiata, the African hero who, despite a very shaky start, led the ancient Mali Empire to glory in the 13th century. Legend has it that Sundiata was part mystic and part visionary. He overcame a childhood disability through his determination to make his mother proud and defend his village from enemies. I hoped my kitten Sundia would turn the tide of my early response to Africa and help me defeat the demons of culture shock.

Striking as a kitten, Sundia had large patches of white and grey on her body and some touches of orange on her face. She was loving and responsive and playful and a much better roommate, I thought, than the two I'd been assigned. Anne, the prim agitated daughter of a nurse, was always fumbling in her oversized medicine bag in search of an antidote for yet another bug bite or upset stomach or mysterious headache. I learned that this was her second try at landing in Africa as a Peace Corps Volunteer.

"Tell them I'm not coming to the meeting today," she moaned from her bed across the boxes on the other side of the room.

"Are you sure? OK," I said, collecting further evidence that she didn't have what it took to last two years here.

Polly, my other roommate and one of the Training Director's favorites, was always just a bit too perky. She'd grown up a law-abiding Catholic, was good at the guitar, could sing on tune and harmonize any melody. Polly was a quick learner and an effective teacher. I was suspicious of her politics from the beginning. She probably hadn't been opposed to the Vietnam War. She must be a Republican, I concluded. I didn't dare ask because I didn't want my hunch confirmed. I had to live with her for a few more weeks.

"Bonjour!" she chirped each morning from her bunk, high above the boxes like mine. She bounced down the ladder, dressed quickly and skipped out the door in her t-shirt and culotte pants. How could I be friends with someone so square? So conservative? She was too much of a goody-goody to be my friend but she sure could sing and play the guitar. Secretly, I envied her musical ability and her fast thinking. I couldn't have landed with roommates more different than myself. So I gravitated to Sundia for solace. She became my *raison d'être* in Lomé. She never got headaches and didn't make me feel inadequate. She had spunk. With Sundia I felt important, competent and appreciated.

Practice-teaching pushed me further to my limits and tested my decision to be an educator. The words of the Peace Corps acceptance letter, once so thrilling and now frankly irksome, reverberated. "You will enjoy the excitement of discovering your own teaching talent." I didn't appear to have teaching talents. The classrooms were little more than boxy concrete spaces with three holes in one wall for windows and a worn-out green chalkboard. No clocks, no bulletin boards, no pictures. The desks were small tables with detached benches that three students shared. Most mornings I looked out over a sea of nearly 70 smooth shaved heads, restless volunteer Togolese English learners. This early training must have been what the letter referred to as "some of the less glamorous aspects of teaching." Less glamorous, indeed! How could I possibly control so many kids in a classroom? I wanted to plead with the students to listen to me, to comply. I did my very best but my teaching talents had yet to emerge.

"Ok, everyone. We're going to review present continuous verb tense. Repeat after me: Koffi is sitting on the bench." When only five of the seventy students responded, I went on to salutations.

"Ok, everyone. We're going to review salutations. Repeat after me: Good morning, Miss Pike! Same pitiful rate of response. Maybe I spoke too quickly, maybe the language was too difficult. I went back to declarative sentences:

"This is a pen. This is a book. What's this, Afua?" I called to a distracted female student in the front row, brandishing a thin *cahier* with a map of Togo on the cover. Still, only five or six students were paying attention. Why had the Director of Training talked about silence? I wanted participation! Christophe and Marçel were kicking a wad of crumpled paper back and forth. Veronique sang softly while twirling the long cylindrical tresses of her girlfriend's hair. Students were not really interested in learning English. I was hopeless as an English teacher in

Africa. The students didn't cooperate, the weather stayed unbearably hot and my enthusiasm waned. I hadn't heard from Denis.

"You won't have trouble when you get to your own school and work with your own students," everyone promised, especially Polly, the carefree Catholic. I envisioned walking into a classroom of still, silent, eager students, books poised open at the correct page, pencils ready to record my instructions. I tried to convince myself it would get easier. I received a surprisingly comforting letter from my stepmom. "By the time you get this, you will probably have changed your mind about Lomé. The people who told you about its beauty were likely looking at it as they left, not when they arrived. Things change more rapidly than we realize." Her advice suggested I think about my attitude towards Lomé and my reservations about her. Could I possibly get used to this? I wondered. In an attempt to force myself out of my misery, I bought the reassurance of my African mentors and friends who'd told me that embracing Africa was the result of getting to know it. *"Afrique, c'est une question d'habitude."*

Happily, there were some auspicious moments. Though Peace Corps volunteers took up most of the rooms at the inn, there were a few intriguing adventurers who passed through and spent the night, sometimes volunteers from other countries, or college grads doing their year around the world on a few cents a day. Sometimes professional trinket collectors appeared. Often American, these "traders" bought beads and cloth in Lomé and resold them to hippies in the States.

"Oooohhhh! Check this out!" we exclaimed at a fresh collection of fabric on display from one of Edith's casual guests.

"The beads are amber and I bought this Coptic cross from a Tuareg on his way north. It must be generations old," the vendor explained, tantalizing us with rare and beautiful objects. The colors and textures whetted my appetite. I couldn't wait to complete training and get out to village markets and search for such treasures on my own. Volunteers clustered around similar distractions many evenings, drinking beer from the German brewery, making jokes about the day's misunderstandings and raving about the range of available French cheeses. "The French know how to choose their colonies!" I moved around the perimeter of the evening huddles, keeping my distance but now resolved to make the best of my stay in Togo as I set my sights on my future life.

Finally, after four tough weeks, practice teaching approached a merciful end. We received our school assignments and prepared to pack up for the last time. The strain of living in close quarters and our impatience to get on with our lives and work frequently collided with good manners. One afternoon after a particularly trying morning of teaching followed by a silent lunch, we returned to our rooms for a brief siesta. Meals were normally lively, but today even canned mackerel sandwiches (Edith's West African version of tuna fish), couldn't budge us out of feeling spent and discouraged. So in the midday heat, Anne, Polly and I settled onto our bunks, weary from the unruly students, the awful food and the frustrations of living with each other's peculiarities. We retreated into our own private worlds, plopped on to our beds and tried to stay cool. Anne and Polly dozed as I lip synched "I feel the earth (pause) move (pause) under my feet, I feel the sky come tumbling down," and resumed my letter-writing.

"Ayyyyyyyyyyyyyyyy!" A sudden high-pitched scream came from Anne's part of the room. I looked up to see Sundia flying at me, feet splayed like a feline bat, kitten-face frozen in terror. Like a furry misshapen grenade, the cat exploded onto my letter, crumpling the tissue paper and poking ragged holes through my careful designs. Polly bolted up alarmed. I lunged to rescue the shaken kitten, cradling her gently and wondering what had happened. I learned that she'd ventured from my bed to Anne's, stalking a cluster of flies. Playfully leaping towards them, she'd landed on Anne's chest. Awakened and scared, Anne grabbed the cat and flung her.

"Why...?!! How could you...?!! NO!" I shouted at Anne.

"Keep your cat away from me!" she spit back, trembling. Then she turned away and pulled the covers over her head, though the temperature must have been somewhere around 100°. I shrugged, shaken too, and determined to have Anne sent home on the spot if my kitten had met serious injury. Climbing down from my bunk I went looking for Edith, restaurateur, hotelier, nurse, and now veterinarian.

"I think she's ok," declared Edith rolling the kitten over in her muscular arms. "A little rattled, but fine. African cats are pretty resilient, like the rest of us here." I was grateful for Edith's assessment, relieved about the kitten but furious at Anne's hostility, replaying the flying cat scene over and over in my mind. I resolved to protect Sundia from my monster roommate for the remaining days of our stay in Lomé.

Spending time exploring Lomé and getting away from Edith's Inn became easier, as I ventured out and about more comfortably. And my increased familiarity on the street enabled me to see beyond first impressions. I could now distinguish many of the different noises during the day: cars, motorbike horns with amusing personalities, chickens, goats, birds and accents from the south and north. I confessed in a letter home that I was going to miss some "little things" about Lomé and described a recent rainstorm:

Yesterday afternoon the bright, sunny sky suddenly filled with dark clouds and a minute later the breeze changed from gentle to forceful until everything, hats, leaves, branches, litter was blowing up, down and over as the rain poured down. The dry, crowded road was instantly flooded and everyone ran helter-skelter in all directions. The storm was followed by a balmy evening of soft, warm air and I looked up beyond the tops of swaying palm trees to a clear, starry sky, feeling peaceful and refreshed.

The day of our departure arrived, capping three months of pedagogical, cultural, linguistic training and anxious anticipation. We looked back at our beginning in northern Quebec and the brief stopovers in Philadelphia, Washington, D.C., and New York for routine medical check-ups, our Peace Corps swearing-in ceremony, and final orientation details. During this initial period, several volunteers had been asked to leave, a few others had left on their own. Those of us who'd made it all the way through, past the bureaucratic delays, the filling-out of endless forms, the medical and dental checks, the many goodbyes to friends and families, the weeks of pre-breakfast language lessons, the interviews to establish our emotional stability, and finally, the torturous practice teaching, were so very relieved to be on our way to our African posts. Our group of trainees, all beginning teachers, was relocating to fifteen different sites.

We were together for the last time, posing for photographs, saying our goodbyes to the trainers and supervisors and to Edith, who waltzed her way through our small crowd with a colorful scarf. My annoyance with her self-assuredness had become amusement. "You're so playful!" I said to Edith in our round of good-byes. She was probably quite relieved to be sending us afar.

I hoped with all my might that Edith's prediction was right, that when we returned to Lomé next we'd be happier and better adjusted.

"I'll be thinking of you all!" she called out, waving her flag-cloth over her head as she danced among us. Perhaps, some day, I would feel as comfortable as Edith appeared to be.

A black creature, a little smaller than my hand, crouched statue-like on the concrete floor. Dad whistled. "Black hairy thick-tailed scorpion," he said, emphasizing each word. "If you can't see a snake on your first day, this is as good as it gets."

—**ROBYN SCOTT**, *Twenty Chickens for a Saddle: The Story of an African Childhood*

MAKING MY WAY: SUSPICIOUS SIGHTINGS

O F ALL THE EARLY FRIENDS I MADE, there was something intriguing, commanding about Christian, Director of Transportation for Peace Corps. He stood tall and straight, at first distinguishing himself in stature. But soon we noticed that it was his character that truly set him apart. Christian was calm and kind. His eyes smiled, even when his mouth didn't, and he was terribly protective of his small staff, as well

Lama-Kara countryside

as of the American administrators who were his colleagues and supervisors. His coworkers referred to him as Le Grand Chef. We all thought of him as *Papa*. He coordinated the drivers and managed a small fleet of vehicles that ventured north, east and west on rutted roads, delivering people and supplies.

The new arrivals, bumbling groups of roughly 15 young Americans, were his self-appointed personal charges, and he watched us with patient amusement as we got lost, fell sick, became discouraged and seemed perpetually confused. We were lucky to have Christian behind us, or more accurately, in front of us, leading the way. He didn't talk much or move fast, but he always got the toughest assignments, for he had proven himself unparalleled at finding remote villages and rescuing people from mishaps. He knew all corners of his country, its languages, cultural imperatives, important people and obscure roads.

"*Attention aux voleurs,*" he advised, alerting us matter-of-factly to the dangers of petty thieves, speeding cars, and mosquitoes. Alarmed at first (*voleurs*? Bandits? Gosh—everyone seemed so nice!), I decided to try to remember Christian's counsel. "Stay alert! Not everyone is as innocent as you believe." Just being around Christian gave us confidence. And lucky for me, he was the driver assigned to take me north and deliver me to my town.

Only Polly, a shiny cross around her neck, and I were sent to live as far away as we requested, well beyond the capital and far from the end of the paved part of the country's one main road. We were assigned to two towns, hers large, mine small, with intermittent electricity (maybe) and almost certainly no running water. We'd been placed in remote posts for two reasons. First, we'd requested locations where we could really be members of our Togolese communities, where there were few other westerners. This Peace Corps goal was first presented in my invitation letter. "You must be willing to learn as well as teach, to realize that you can do a better job of teaching your students when you understand not just the part of their lives as represented by the school compound, but also their heritage as represented by both the towns and villages of their childhood and the families who reared them." I couldn't wait to learn about my students' backgrounds. I assumed a second reason Polly and I were sent far away was because we were independent, strong and healthy, and we wouldn't require "handholding" by Peace Corps support staff, the supervision of medical assistants or the regular company of other Americans.

"Please put me in a school as far away from the capital city as possible," I begged the Country Peace Corps Director at our initial meeting. I remained embarrassed by my country's role in the Vietnam War. If I lived way up north, my Togolese friends would not associate me with the American Embassy, the Peace Corps office, or Edith's Inn. "I'm in Africa to be with Africans, learn African ways," I wrote in letters to friends and family members. "I hope to be the only American in my town."

So I was heading 400 kilometers north, roughly 250 miles, cast afield with just one other American: my Lomé roommate Polly, who played the guitar and sang songs only my grandparents knew, who had mastered teaching from the first day (even with classes of seventy students), and who had never made a single misbehaving step in her 20-something years. Her hair bounced when she walked, she didn't have to struggle to stay thin, and she knew how to say teeth in Serbo-Croatian, an early clue that she would have no trouble with local languages. She never questioned silly rules or rigid lesson plan guides. My new friend, nearest colleague in geographical terms, and potential confidante was the epitome of Miss Goody-Goody and I had to learn to like her. Well then, I would have to convince her to want to live like a Togolese. She wouldn't be seeing much of me if she chose to hang out on tennis courts with ex-patriots.

Like all Africans living in countries strung along the Gold Coast, Polly and I quickly learned that Togolese spoke at least three languages. They used one to greet and converse with relatives, another to travel and a third to shop. And most people spoke two or three additional languages that connected them to their parents' and grandparents' heritage. People thought nothing of being multilingual. We were in awe of such linguistic versatility and I resolved from the start to learn greetings in as many languages as regions I planned to visit. I made friends swiftly to speed up my efforts.

"*Alafia-we!*"

"*Ufoa?*"

"*Nwale,*" I alternated saying simple greetings in Kabré, Kotokoli and Ewe. I mastered the first few words but then reached my limit and reverted to French.

"*Eh oui, Françis! Bonjour!*" I tried to learn so much in the early days, wrapping my tongue around vowel blends I didn't know existed, abiding by the cultural demands to greet people in such a prescriptive way, the hand-shaking, the smiling, the ritual of acknowledging the ancestors. I tried to remember that *bon soir* was not the same as *bonne nuit,* that gender and conjugation mistakes were generously forgiven and that everywhere everyone appreciated attempts at speaking one of the local languages, even if done poorly. Whenever we had a chance, Polly and I tossed greetings in different languages back and forth. She was as eager as I was to learn local expressions.

For the trip north, I'd fashioned a cage out of cardboard to contain my kitten, Sundia, though I hoped to hold her on my lap during most of the truck ride. With everyone's help, Polly and I loaded bags and boxes onto Christian's large truck, carefully wedging my brand new guitar and shortwave radio between suitcases for protection. The early morning was unusually clear and cool and the sun was bright as Polly and I pushed and pulled each other into the cabin. Perhaps Lomé was as happy at our departure as we were leaving, tossing this group of confused and whiny Westerners to other towns and villages, where locals could assume responsibility for our comfort. And welcoming they were bound to be, as we'd experienced the generosity of Togolese hospitality in our encounters during training.

Christian started the engine and it bellowed and shuddered, buffeting us against each other. The truck squeaked and groaned as it leaned and bumped its way away from Edith's Inn. We waved out the open windows, trying not to inhale truck exhaust, and called out good-byes in as many languages as we could remember. Finally, finally, finally.

It was going to take two or three days of travel to reach our final destination, my town of Lama-Kara, with an overnight stop along the way to deliver Polly. We followed an indirect route north because Christian had to deliver supplies to another volunteer in Palimé, a mid-sized town about an hour north of Lomé on a road that wound its way through lush green

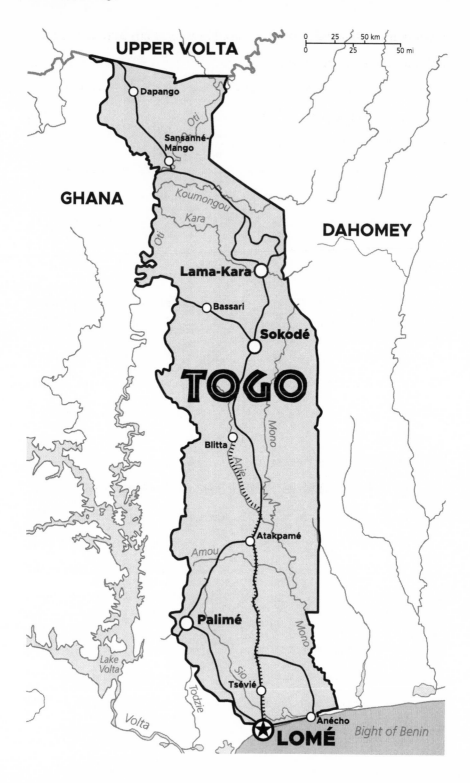

mountains. Just outside the town, we came upon a large group of people walking to a silent rhythm in the middle of the street. Four men were at the front holding a platform above their heads. *"C'est une funeraille,"* Christian explained. It was a funeral. The body of the deceased lay on the platform, wrapped in many meters of bright white cloth. Behind the men marched fifty or so women. I noticed that a few of the women seemed bored, unaffected. Others were in various manifestations of grief, some crying, others moaning, wailing or screaming. I couldn't take my eyes off the bizarre sight. Christian explained that dying in West Africa was met with grief and joy. Joy when someone dies?

"People who have died can now meet the loved ones who've passed on before. They are intermediaries between visible and invisible worlds. And with a proper funeral they achieve their life's goal: to become ancestors!" Peering out the truck window, Polly and I watched the procession as it receded in the distance. We struggled to understand what Christian had explained. Losing a loved one can be cause for celebration?

Our lumbering truck passed through villages every twenty minutes or so, where we stopped to buy fruit or wave back to children who jumped and danced and shouted *"Bonjour! Bonjour! Bonjour!"* by the side of the road. There was thunder, lightning, rain, then bright sun and clear blue sky as we continued, trundling our way north, watching the colors of the earth change from red to orange to brown to beige, and admiring purple mountains silhouetted by silver-gray clouds.

Sundia mostly behaved herself, sleeping on my lap until we came to a stop or a rutted patch of road where she was startled awake and squirmed to escape my grip. Christian always tried to take holes, mounds, sudden turns gently, warning me ahead of time.

"*Tiens bien!*" he advised me to hold the kitten with one hand and the dashboard with the other, signaling a hazard.

"Do you want me to take the kitten?" offered Polly. "If you're uncomfortable, we can trade places." I was happy that she tolerated my preoccupation with the kitten. Perhaps she wasn't a Republican. Everyone seemed filled with optimism and generosity.

We reached Polly's post in Sokodé and her new home by mid-afternoon on the second day. Christian introduced us to the large town by driving around sharp bends and through narrow passageways to greet friends and acquaintances. I noted that it wasn't as crowded as southern towns. There were fewer people and hardly any cars. Women walked purposefully, carrying large bundles and usually leading a line of small children. Men strode by in groups of two or three, arms joined, wearing long gowns, *boubous* of light blue or white, always with small crocheted caps on their heads. Sokodé was the largest Muslim community in Togo. There appeared to be considerable religious tolerance among the diverse communities we passed through, but I knew very little about what people believed and practiced. I assumed most people managed to balance more than one set of beliefs simultaneously, animism most prominent in rural regions overlaid with Christianity or Islam, or both. Colonialists from Europe and Moslem traders across the desert had done their work of teaching Togolese that it was prudent to pray to many gods. Everyone appeared friendly. Our driver, Christian, was immediately recognized and exuberantly greeted by the townspeople walking about. They called out as we arrived.

Christian let out a cheerful shout, turned off the engine, descended from his seat, and proceeded to greet the many small clusters of men in the local language Kotokoli through an exchange of greetings that continued for nearly twenty back-and-forths.

Un-la-waa lay! (Good morning!)

Yaa. Alafia. (Yes, it is good.)

Alafia-we? (Are you good?)

Alafia. (Fine.)

Tomiai yo? (How's your work?)

Alafia.

Halo yo? (How's your wife?) or

Pay-way Alafia? (How are your wives?)

Alafia.

Pia yo? (And your children?)

Alafia.

Plab-tassi. (See you later.)

Plab-tassi.

Ungh

Unn

Ungh

Unn

Ungh

Unn

Ungh

Unn

Polly and I listened, trying to memorize the rhythmic sequence, but our giddiness made it impossible to get beyond the second *Alafia*. It sounded so odd and repetitive, and we tried to stifle our amusement. The gutteral utterances from grown men elegantly dressed seemed so peculiar.

Back in the truck after a long pause of multiple greetings, we pulled up to a recently completed building. Christian parked and turned off the engine as the vehicle shook and shuddered to silence. I peered out the window. Could this be Polly's house? It looked like a customs station where officials stamped passports. No, a clinic where young nurses treated despondent babies. This couldn't be Polly's house, could it? It was modern (door knobs, cabinet handles, windows), new (crisp corners, smooth walls), completely empty (except for some bits and pieces of cement that hadn't yet been swept away) and too big to be anything but a headquarters for foreigners. This must have been the brainstorm of a prosperous Togolese builder who had cleverly predicted the arrival of French and American aid workers. A concrete wall surrounded the house. There was even a toilet. A toilet?! An installed sink in the kitchen suggested the possibility of running water. Wow! Polly was going to live in Africa like she lived in the States. The only signs of life were the young papaya and banana trees off to the side of the house, next to the wall. The house was quiet and impersonal and smelled tinny, of recently mixed concrete.

"How lucky you are to be living in a new place," I said to Polly, trying to reassure her, pretending not to be disappointed. No way was I going to live in similar quarters! I'd move to a mud house in the bush before I'd live like this. This isn't how Africans live! Once again, I asked Christian to confirm that I'd be living in a compound with Togolese neighbors, not in my own house, and that I'd be living as they lived.

"*Oui, Mademoiselle,*" he repeated with a slight smirk. "*C'est sûr.*" He reminded me that I wouldn't have running water or electricity. It sounded wonderful to me. As we walked from room to room in Polly's house, people approached from all directions to welcome us and help us unload. I secured Sundia in a corner where she wouldn't run away and we began carting boxes and bags inside. The warm welcome and enthusiastic assistance thawed my early wariness of Polly's new home. After a string of introductions and explanations, most of which confused me, people drifted off, the sun set and Polly and I prepared to settle in for the night. Christian left to stay with friends closer to the center of town.

"Let's practice our new songs on the guitar. Let's fill this space with music!" Polly proposed, warding off, I suspected, some early fears of loneliness. Melodies would override the discomfort. We planted ourselves on the hard cement floor, sitting upon new *pagnes*, brightly colored pieces of African cloth, shifting our positions to stay comfortable. We sang hymns and folk songs, our voices echoing off freshly whitewashed walls in empty rooms. In the mostly dark house, we held matches to coils to keep mosquitoes away, watching the smoke spiral upward. They added their overly perfumed fragrance to the metallic smells of nails and sand and helped us feel sure that this precaution, along with the strong pills we were taking, would prevent malaria. Between songs, we wrote in our journals recording the trip north and sketching Polly's new home. We practiced the local Kotokoli greetings, usually collapsing in laughter before we got to the end. We pledged to stay in touch every week by sending messages to each other through friends traveling back and forth or with the occasional (and costly) phone call. Up until now, our ages, styles, and backgrounds had set us apart. Now we were eager to find similarities, young women in distant outposts.

The next morning Christian arrived with the first light as a nearby cock crowed. He and I prepared to leave Sokodé on the journey's last leg. We made cups of instant coffee with Polly's triple gas burner "stove" and ate fresh bread with soft fat triangles of Vache Qui Rit cheese, taking in tasty bites of spongy cheese and refreshing morning air standing outside beside the small papaya tree. I envisioned a few months in the future, climbing the nearby wall to harvest plump papayas. The *muezzin* sang out the call to prayer from an adjacent mosque.

Breakfast eaten, I walked into the small bathroom to wash my face and suddenly retracted my hands from the spigot. There was a huge black spider crawling slowly toward me. Ewwwww! Looking more closely I saw that it was hairy, with front pinchers and a malevolent-looking tail curling over its back. A scorpion!

"Christian! *Viens*!! Come quickly! PLEASE!" I shouted. He hastened into the bathroom, spotted the enormous black bug and "POW!" with the heel of his shoe whacked the venomous insect dead.

"Yikes! I can't believe it! I could have been stung by a scorpion and I haven't even gotten to my new home!!" I exclaimed dramatically. I'd never seen a scorpion before, but knew that they were not uncommon here. And though they looked menacing and could even kill, I'd overheard in a conversation at Edith's Inn that ancient Egyptians believed scorpions were good luck. Are they good or bad? Are funerals sad or happy? So much of what I knew to be true was being turned upside down. I wondered if I should have encouraged Christian to let the scorpion go free. Was the scorpion a premonition? Or a sign of good things to come?

"Scorpions are dangerous," Christian told me. "We always kill them on sight." I comforted myself by believing that simply spotting the scorpion had brought me good luck.

While we'd been dealing with the scorpion, a group of young men had arrived with furniture and Polly was directing them to arrange beds, tables and chairs. Christian oversaw the operation and turned to address me. "I've had a *communiqué* with folks in your town, Mademoiselle, and they are cleaning your house and bringing furniture too. They're waiting for us." I clapped my hands with eagerness to learn where I'd be living.

"Are you ready to go?" he asked. "Oh, yes!" I practically shouted. I finished putting away some bowls and plates on shelves in the kitchen, then called Polly over, gave her a hug and asked if she'd be comfortable settling in without us. After all, I thought, this would be the first time in three months we'd be on our own. We hugged again, our lively energy revealing enthusiasm, fear, uncertainty, excitement as I made my way to the truck, grabbing the kitten and clambering up and in. Both Christian and I waved good-bye to the group gathered 'round us. "Let me know how you like your new home!" Polly called as we drove away. Now I really, finally, felt as if I were off on my adventure.

"How long until we arrive, Christian?"

"Not long, Mademoiselle," his eyes hinted a smile.

The next section of road was bumpy but dry, so it took us only an hour. Without large puddles to dodge, the trip was shorter than imagined. All the way from Lomé, I'd watched with fascination as the earth had changed colors. Roadside trees and bushes were scant now, definitely not the lush tropical zone we'd come from farther south. The air had changed too, lifting from humid, warm, heavy to dry and breezy. Looking out the windshield, kitten comfortably nestled in my lap, I peered across expanses of rolling hills dotted with leafy *manguiers* and slim *palmiers* standing royal and solitary. They encircled dwellings with cylindrical straw roofs. Beyond the clusters of small structures, green fields of millet and grass covered the hills. How beautiful it was! I was going to be living surrounded by these rolling hills, eating from these fields and living like the people who had roamed this region for millenia.

Christian explained that my house was in the center of town. I'd be sharing a compound with several other Togolese families. Perfect! We entered the town by crossing the Kara River then pulled up in front of a large marketplace, an open concrete platform sheltered by sheets of

Entrance to Lama-Kara

corrugated tin. Christian explained that the name of my town, Lama-Kara, meant the village Lama beside the river Kara. People had told me that its 10,000 inhabitants made it a significant northern center of commerce.

"This is not market day," Christian continued. But I spotted plenty of people moving about on the dirt roads, women carrying bundles of firewood, baskets of gourds, babies, bins of brightly-colored plastic pitchers. A few men drove by in a large truck, other men motored past on *mobylettes*, small motorized bicycles whining under the strain of two or even three passengers. Young people rode bicycles, also in twos or threes and sometimes with young passengers swinging their short legs from handlebars. Everyone stopped to stare as Christian and I drove by. I returned their stares and smiled, just as curious and wide-eyed as they were.

We pulled into my compound slowly, Christian navigating carefully in order to avoid the children, chickens and dogs that darted and scurried in all directions. The hulking truck came to a stop directly across from the marketplace, in the middle of an unwalled common area, where I looked over to see a small group of people, young and old, local and foreign, busily sweeping, wiping down walls and carrying furniture into what I suspected was my home. As I got out of the truck, a boy of about eleven dressed in shorts only, no shirt or shoes, ran up to me.

"*Mees? Mees?*" He called me "Miss" and reached to take one of the bags from my hand to assist me. "*Je suis Sina. Je vais travailler pour vous.*" His name was Sina and he said he would be working for me. I smiled and tried to tell him we'd talk about that later, but I wasn't sure what I said or what he heard. I felt nervous about having someone work for me especially when I didn't get a chance to choose who that would be. I handed him another bag and tried not to feel overwhelmed. Was I going to have a boy working for me? If so, I liked his take-charge manner. Or did I? Was he too pushy? I inhaled, and decided that I'd handle it all later. First I wanted to check out where I'd be living. I walked forward, clutching Sundia and a bag.

"Hello!"

"You made it!"

"*Bonjour Mees Pike!*"

"Welcome!"

"*Bienvenue!*"

"*Alafia-we!*"

Strangers ran down the steps of my house and greeted me with hugs, handshakes and bows as I approached. They were Americans visiting from outlying villages, neighbors and compound-mates. My new home was a three-room suite, at the far end of a long block of connected rooms, neighbor to several (three? four?) local families. I learned that I'd be sharing the latrine and cooking and eating areas with them.

"*Sina, s'il vous plaît, où est la latrine?*" Did I have a toilet like Polly?

"*Latrine, Mees? Oui! Là-bas!*" Sina pointed to the far end of our compound, across a field surrounding the living space. Near the road about twenty-five feet from my rooms, I spotted a tall aluminum-sided structure obscured by large leggy plants. "*Voilà, Mees. Ça c'est la latrine.*" No toilet and no running water. What a relief! I would truly be living like an African.

Flanked by my court of greeters, I walked up the three steps into my suite, through crooked wooden doors. I followed everyone's lead and kicked off my leather sandals, dusty from the long trip and the dirt floor of the compound. I felt the smooth coolness of the bare concrete floor of my new living room. It was a contrast to the floor at Polly's house, where scratchy bits of cement kept getting stuck in our toes. I took in the soft yellow light of the empty space as I walked through the rooms. Everything felt well-loved, seasoned, welcoming, homey.

"*Et voila, Mademoiselle. Qu'est-ce que vous en pensez?*" Christian wanted to know if I liked my small home.

"It's beautiful, Christian! It's perfect!" Could I explain to him that the best part was that I was living among Africans? I was living like Africans! I hoped we'd eat together in our shared space. I'd learn their ways, venture into their language, acquire skills I never imagined! The "greeting committee", new friends, had already installed a wooden bed and were draping a gauzy mosquito net over each of the posts. There was a screened wooden closet next to the bed and a few cushions on the floor.

Christian walked through my rooms several times eyeing a corner for my bookcase, a wall for my desk and an arrangement for a dish cabinet and my water filter in the kitchen. He suggested a screen door for the entryway and asked the landlord, my immediate neighbor who had come to welcome me, to take some measurements. He instructed a couple of the helpers to visit the carpenter the next day and have him build a desk, a couple of chairs, and a table with two large holes for the basins that would be my kitchen "sinks." We made a few more preliminary arrangements, planning new doors and a space for a small garden. Everybody was helping. Sina's older cousin was going to deliver water from the river each morning at dawn, once the rain ceased. I was reminded to boil and filter it before drinking. A heavy ceramic water filter sat on the only table.

Christian watched as I settled my bags and boxes, and then he prepared to leave. We escorted him out to the truck and I thanked him in as many languages as I could conjure up.

"*Au revoir! A bientot! Merci! Akpe! Akpe ka ka!*" I called and waved as he maneuvered the truck out of our compound. I felt nervous at Christian's departure but excited, too, to be on my own.

The group of greeters and I went back inside and settled in my new African living room, arranging colorful pagnes when we ran out of cushions to sit on. It felt so good. The home was clean and refreshing. My new friends had brought oranges and bananas that we passed around, peeling the thin skins and releasing a citrusy sweetness into the afternoon warmth. The sun beamed in, illuminating this happy circle on the smooth cement floor. I was finally home.

> Schoolteaching was perfect for understanding how people lived and what they wanted for themselves. And my work justified my existence in Africa. I had never wanted to be a tourist. I wished to be far away, as remote as possible, among people I could talk to.
>
> —**PAUL THEROUX**, *Dark Star Safari*

TEACHING IN TOGO

MY WORK BEGAN in the bosom of the Catholic Church, for I was assigned to teach English in a girls' parochial school run by six European nuns. I'd be teaching adolescents, roughly the equivalent of high school ages, and was following a queue of former volunteers who had completed their two years' service. Surely, they were joking, I thought to myself when the Peace Corps Director first announced that **I** was the volunteer selected to teach at Collège Sainte Adèle. The school had been

Collège Adèle students

established by Catholic missionaries nearly a decade earlier. Me? In a Catholic school? Teaching with nuns? Struggling between relief and disbelief, delighted to move beyond training, but stunned at my assignment, I decided to trust the wisdom of the Peace Corps and accept this fate. Perhaps it was karma at work, some sort of comic payback for my disdain of anything the Pope in Rome represented to me. As a teenager in the 60's, suspicious of authority in any form, I'd disapproved of Catholic assumptions that we'd been born sinners, that birth control was wrong, and that only men could be priests.

Ha! I laughed aloud thinking about how my mother and I would now have tales to share. She was teaching in a Catholic school in northern California and had adopted an authority I found unfamiliar. She seemed more decisive, more sure of herself, less flexible. What was it about religion that made adults autocratic? In pre-Africa conversations with my mom, I'd expressed surprise at her school's rigidity. But instead of agreeing with me and resenting her superiors, she defended them. I was aghast. She'd toughened over the years, and was considered to be the best disciplinarian in the school. I was surprised when parents began requesting that their kids be placed in her class. Perhaps my experience in Africa would toughen me, make me really good at something too. An expert in warming the chill of a Catholic education in Africa? An expert in convincing young Togolese women that they deserved to be educated? An expert in outsmarting rigid authority structures? Certainly there would be redemption in this Catholic immersion experience.

But even with an open mind, I confessed that my teaching assignment at Collège Adèle lacked authenticity. Fresh out of training and yearning to learn regional languages and adopt local values and practices, I feared my teaching assignment would prevent "community integration" rather than foster it. All along, I'd imagined that I'd be placed in a typically large public school. Now I saw stark contrasts. At Collège Adèle, I traipsed across the open courtyard catching the mottled shade of jacaranda and mimosa trees instead of threading my way between teachers and students in the humid echo-filled halls of a crowded Togolese government-run high school. I'd be learning more about how the French Catholic church adapted itself in hardship posts than watching the ongoing operation of a Togolese school. And instead of working alongside earnest African colleagues, my colleagues were six European nuns. "Classrooms are clean, chalkboards are legible, and there's a book for (almost) every student," I wrote in letters home, fending off disappointment. Surely there were perks to this assignment. Uncommon in other schools, the students had study materials, there were lots of extra holidays and I had access to the nuns' sewing machine. Yes, definite perks.

The women who ran Collège Adèle, a high school in spite of its name, dressed in oversized long sleeved white robes and moved about constantly. Usually silent and solitary, they wove through the courtyard on a crisscross of paths, ducking under and around the trimmed trees, working their way back and forth to the office building. They passed girls huddled in clusters, students covered in colorful drapes of cloth emitting joyful noises never quite contained. The nuns seemed scornful of such lively energy as they brushed past with disapproving clucks and glares. The school buildings were neat and orderly, the cement floors and whitewashed walls bare and cold. Tidy but colorless. Classrooms were airy and light, built strategically around a frequently scrubbed chapel. Off to the side of a courtyard was the long, two-story office building that sat at an oblique angle to the rest of the school. The few manicured trees in the courtyard were so frequently trimmed that they altogether missed blooming seasons. The jacaranda and mimosa were permitted to send out little buds, but as soon as blooming began, just before they burst into color, blossoms were snapped off. The sanitized, sterile setting intimidated me.

As for the students at Collège Adèle, they were a sharp contrast to the school compound and the nuns in charge. They flashed friendly smiles and jumped or skipped or gathered in a group embrace at the slightest provocation. These girls were considered lucky. It took some maneuvering to be admitted to the school, usually on the part of an older brother or generous uncle with some extra money and a place to live not far away. Most students were older than they claimed to be, having lived long enough to appreciate how a high school education could propel them beyond punishing lives as cooks, childcare workers and housemaids. On their way to elevated roles as privileged, educated Togolese women, these girls took care of their appearance, usually dressing in beautiful outfits of bright colors, wearing modest jewelry that glittered or bounced or shone brightly against their smooth dark skin. All the locals knew about the beautiful girls from *Adèle*, and were impressed when I told them where I was teaching.

In order to prepare myself for working with only girl students, I read and reread an information sheet I was given by a Togolese "culture expert" during our training.

Togolese are very hospitable. In order to be considered hospitable and warm, a Togolese tries to find a wife who is calm, not very talkative, and respectful—in other words, well-educated…Traditionally, when a family receives a visitor, members of the family run to him to carry his belongings or whatever he may have on his head or in his hands.

First and foremost, they give the visitor water to drink. This is generally done by the wife. Thus, you can see why one must have a pleasant and friendly wife.

A wife who doesn't talk much and knows when to serve water is educated?! Such a definition of "educated" took me by surprise and I resolved to see if this played out in my region. So far, the Togolese women I'd met hardly seemed submissive. Just the opposite! Yes, in the early days my students worked hard in class to avoid the wrath of the nuns. But in the courtyard, they were loud and exuberant and couldn't resist sharing gossip.

"Can you believe it??!!"

"Did you hear?!!"

"*Çe n'est pas vrai!!*" they took turns refusing to believe what one or another of them had announced.

"What about Véronique's uncle? He's in love with the President's cousin!"

"Marcelline's not coming back!"

"I think she got married!"

"I heard she got pregnant!"

Though I wasn't privy to most of their stories, I got to know the girls quickly, remembering the pronunciation of everyone's name, the Euphrasies and Rakiétous a cheerful challenge. I could recognize students' distinct voices, Justine's lilting sing-song narratives, Marie-Laurent's

Marcelline and Sister Lorenca

sensational outbursts, Claudine's tsks of disapproval. Their beauty and enthusiasm surrounded me at school and charmed me. I wanted to speak French like these girls, look like these girls. Mariama held her tall body upright and smiled with her whole face. She was alert and attentive. Euphrasie had complicated hair sculptures: braids that turned and twisted in graceful formations about her small face. She was more timid than her classmates and cast her head downward when spoken to, providing many opportunities to study her intricate hair patterns. Rakiétou wrapped multi-colored pagnes about her waist and shoulders, displaying fresh new batik patterns that set off her shapely form and graceful flowing style. Maybe teaching in a girls' school wasn't so bad.

The nuns, on the other hand, were at first indistinguishable. They dressed alike. They walked alike, darting from office to classroom and back again with brisk, purposeful steps. And though their heights and accents differed, they all spoke really fast, in lightning-speed French that was so intimidating I couldn't understand what they said. I couldn't even remember their names at the beginning. But beyond their common blur of incomprehensible language and billowing white shapes, there was a symmetry about these sisters that gave them definition. They came in pairs: two from Spain, two from France, two from Italy. I finally learned to tell them apart by listening and watching carefully when they spoke. The nuns from Spain stretched their vowels and talked through easy smiles. The two from Italy added syllables to words and ended every sentence with a rise in intonation. I was never sure if they were querying me or commanding me. The two from France were a bizarre couple: *la première*, Sister Marie-Bertille, was short and wide with shiny wisps of white hair that tried desperately to escape the habit that so tightly framed her round fleshy face. Although she looked ill and misshapen beside the dark, sleek African students she taught, she had a sweet smile and forgiving nature, so I went to her most often when I had questions about grading requirements or schedule changes.

La deuxième, her compatriot, was fierce. Sister Kathérine was la Soeur Directrice, director, principal, overseer. She had dark, beadlike eyes that peered out from under spare, pointy eyebrows. Her stiff, puckered lips never smiled. Her lookout pose, a permanent facial expression, was held in place by a taut, relentless scowl. When she spoke it was high-pitched, serious and usually a reprimand. There were any number of transgressions students made, so I never saw Sister Kathérine relaxed or happy, or even mildly pleased. She and I were to meet at the end of each term to discuss students' grades. I was already dreading these end-of-term conferences and prepared weeks in advance, not by reviewing students' progress, but by practicing a fast-paced version of French. I wondered if La Soeur Directrice was out to get me using French as her weapon. At the beginning, I was convinced that the smirk she failed to hide during our conversations was her satisfaction at having sped up her French to such a rate that I was left tripping over verb tenses or whimpering for the fourth time, *"C'est quoi, ma Soeur? Je n'ai pas très bien compris."* I just couldn't understand what she said. She and all the nuns were usually polite to me, so I was confused by the severity of their behavior in front of students.

My casual California style provided my nun-colleagues, particularly la Soeur Kathérine, some fertile ground for stern pedagogical training. They took opportunities to help me.

"Stop those students from talking!"

"Those little beasts—DON'T let them take advantage of you!"

"They only respond to commands. Give them orders!"

"You mustn't be so nice!"

From their perspective, I was way too lenient. I smiled too often, talked too much and was way too congenial. From my end, I loved these girls from the beginning and did not hide my delight at working with them every day. They were fun and lively and much better students than the volunteer students I'd practiced with in Lomé. I found the nuns' approach hostile, even cruel. I didn't follow their advice. Being mean will never work, I decided. But my attempts to establish order didn't work.

Me: (Clapping to get my thirty or so students' attention.) I shouted out, "Good morning, students!"

Students: (After three repetitions, they replied.) "Good morrrning, Mees!"

Me: "Please turn to page 27." (I nodded, trying to establish eye contact with the most talkative ones, and smiled.)

Students: (Continued conversations, laughter)

Me: "Please turn to page 27."

Students in the first row only slowly put textbooks on desks and began, sloth-like, to look for page 27. All other students continued chattering.

Me: "Ladies!" I lowered my voice, furrowed my eyebrows and pretended to be annoyed. "Turn to page 27."

On some mornings, students stopped gossiping because they simply ran out of small talk or they were curious to proceed with the lesson. On other mornings, one of the nuns walked in, having heard the clamor. It was usually la Soeur Kathérine. She appeared out of nowhere, her scowl and silence more menacing than ever. The students and I froze in humiliation, each silently blaming the other for this wicked nun's ability to ruin a promising day. I planted my feet on the floor and stood up taller, hoping that upright posture would belie my lack of class control. But students exchanged knowing smiles at this empty gesture and Soeur Kathérine finally walked out, to my relief, thoroughly disgusted by both students and their incompetent teacher.

So it was the students' moods and whims that largely determined the success of my classes in the early days. Random outbursts or devious whispering easily confounded the clearest of grammar lessons or dissolved a dialogue drill. Eventually, though, having lost patience with students' noisy restlessness and having observed the severity of the nuns, I began retracting smiles and worked on perfecting a more effective scowl.

"Justine and Marie-Hélène will stop talking," I said, suddenly serious, my voice uncharacteristically even.

"Mariama! Please tell all of us what you just said to Rakiétou." At first

Collège Adèle colleagues

they laughed. Mees is getting angry! But these small disciplinary strategies started to succeed and students began to take me more seriously. I threatened more homework, kept misbehaving students after class and singled out those who weren't keeping up. I was becoming another nun, I scoffed. I hated the teacher I was becoming. But it worked.

My teaching schedule included four levels of English and three levels of art, with French textbooks for English and nothing, no manuals or supplies, for art. I was left to dream up activities for this class and scavenge whatever materials followed the dream, which wasn't so bad for someone who loved crafts. But teaching English was another story—it was much more difficult—and lesson prep was never-ending. It improved when I got better at designing lessons that were packed with activities. I adapted chapters on topics far from students' understanding and experience, as we were working from textbooks that came from Paris. The readings on snowstorms, pet rabbits and symphony orchestras became vocabulary lessons for sandstorms, African geography and local holidays. My teaching got better as first weeks became first months. If my lessons were fast-paced and full of variety, I usually had attentive students. But it was exhausting. Teaching, I decided, was a lesson-by-lesson proposition. So I tried to make each lesson relevant and fun. Yes, it was exhausting.

I had classes all morning then returned home for lunch. After a three-hour siesta, I went back to school for two more hours of class, finishing up around 5. The sun set an hour later, so I had scant daylight to prepare lessons for the next day or cook dinner. I tried both by the light of my kerosene lanterns.

"Mees! Mees! *Venez, dinez avec nous!*" George called from the common area in our compound, inviting me to share some fresh okra stew with the other compound families.

"Sorry, George. *Trop de travail!*" I called out, claiming that I had too much work to join them.

Honestly, most evenings it was nearly impossible to concentrate, the acrid scent of lantern fuel burning my eyes and irritating my nose. And there were insects of all sizes humming about my perspiring body or buzzing straight into the glow of the lamp. Some hit glass and burned on contact. Others imitated the flight patterns of survivors and buzzed away. I turned my face away from the sights and smells to take in the much more pleasant fragrance of wafting *citronelle*, lemongrass bushes beyond the compound, or the fragrant evening wood smoke from nearby fires. I daydreamed about friends and family at home. I wondered when my mobylette would arrive, when I'd see Polly next and why I'd never heard from Denis. Had I given him the right address? Had he forgotten about me as soon as I'd dropped out of sight? I received mail only twice a week, Tuesdays and Fridays, so maybe his letter had been delayed. I tried to stay focused on my work, making sure my cat had been fed and ignoring the clatter of children outside talking, washing dishes, sweeping dirt floors of our shared space, or hailing villagers who walked past on an evening stroll. But it was usually too hard to tune out the sounds. I caught myself trying to translate conversations, making guesses about who was talking or what they were talking about. I replayed interactions in French or missteps in class from earlier in the day. I vowed to stop saying *bizarre* so frequently and be more concise at giving students directions.

There was so much to distract me from endless prep in the evenings. After not finishing the next day's planning, or scoring student work, or reviewing the textbook lesson, I gave up. Feeling defeated by the disturbances, the survival drama of the insects, my exhaustion and the frustration of trying to work in such challenging circumstances, I headed for bed. My kitten followed me, jumped on the pillows, wedging herself under the mosquito net without pulling or tearing it, as I leaned over to blow out the kerosene lamp, and together, as the scent of lemongrass drifted through the open window, we fell asleep.

Everyone is curious. Everyone stares at the white woman coming out of her house... The children stop playing to look. The students living in the hut next door stand up from their washing and stop to watch me. The neighbors, bending over in their peanut fields, hands deep in soil, wave, and wipe away the sweat from their foreheads and necks...As soon as the women see me, they stop laughing. They stop playing, and they stop washing. They don't do anything. They just stare at me.

—**SUSANA HERRERA**, *Mango Elephants in the Sun*

THE THRONE: UPS AND DOWNS

Dear Jo and Daddyo,

Things are going very well here. I've been teaching for a few weeks now and it feels as if it's been six months! The students pay attention and my nun-colleagues are nice to me. The campus is full of trees and flowers and the classrooms are clean.

The "Throne"

I was upbeat and happily surprised by my students' increased engagement. I knew I'd have bad days, but teaching was getting to be fun. In spite of the many hours required to prepare lessons, correct exercises and design tests, I was refining my techniques and I loved being on my own. I taught six days a week, every day but Sunday, English in the mornings and one or two art classes in the afternoon. Walking to and from school was sometimes the most entertaining part. In the early mornings the weather was cool, and I could catch glimpses of light purple mountains in the distance and brilliant white clouds sliding across a bright blue sky. Everyone I passed greeted me with a *"Bonjour, Madame!"* or *"N'liowe!"* I was too timid to reply to the Kabré. The sounds got all mixed up in my mouth and I feared I'd sputter out something silly, so I just smiled and nodded. The women giggled at my self-consciousness and continued on their way, transporting huge bundles of wood or plastic pots or stacks of fabric on their heads. My route took me past several neighbor compounds. When children spotted me, they'd start jumping up and down, singing, dancing, hugging each other and shouting *"Yovo! Yovo!"* They ran up to me, grabbed whatever I was carrying, usually a bag of books and teaching aids, plopped it all atop their heads and on we walked together. Their eagerness pulled me out of anxiety about the upcoming morning's lessons.

At day's end, if I didn't have lessons to plan when I returned home, I'd grab a snack and practice chords on my guitar or chitchat with the compound children in a mixture of French, Kabré and gestures. There were about a dozen kids, from newborn to teen living in the compound, and they were all fascinated by me and my stuff. Whenever I was home, they knocked on my rickety front door, walked inside (invited or not), picked up a broom and started sweeping. One afternoon when I was washing dishes, Afia came into the kitchen, took the sponge and plate from my hands without a word, and proceeded to wash the dishes. Wow! When my water supply ran low, the kids brought me full buckets from a nearby well, a ten-minute walk away. And nearly always, the older children accompanied me to the market. In the early days, I shopped for household supplies, curtain fabric, pots to place between the boards for my bookcase, matches for the kerosene lamps and whatever fresh produce was available. The kids helped me carry everything home, as we'd march home in a colorful and widely-observed procession, directly across the street.

Living right smack in the center of town was convenient, but I began to realize just how public it was. It was so central that the weekly market overflowed into my millet field. Most days we'd peer at a large mostly abandoned concrete platform sheltered by a huge corrugated tin roof. But on market day, fruit and vegetable growers came from the south, African bead merchants came from the north, and local peddlers of boxed matches, canned tomato sauce, onions and batteries converted the empty space to a day-long festival venue. Our part of town became an enormous vibrant block party and to most shoppers, after the shopping and socializing at the market, our compound, so open and visible, was the main event.

Living so publicly was challenging. To neighbors from town or visitors from outlying villages, my fair skin and long blonde hair was a curiosity. When I stepped outside my two rooms, everyone stopped and stared. Argh. People were really curious. I tried to be understanding about the gawkers. It seemed less hostile than it had felt in Lomé, but I still felt self-conscious. Planting flower seeds in my tiny garden or walking to the nearby provisions store had me hesitating, wondering how many gapers I'd entertain. I imagined the momentary apprehension a movie star faces before going on stage. Sometimes it was excruciating. I learned to organize the day's activities by grouping them into interior (don't have to go outside) and exterior (I have to go outside), steeling myself, screwing up my resolve for as long as fifteen minutes before embarking on the outside list. I'd been taught not to stare, so it seemed terribly invasive and impolite when others stared at me. My self-consciousness made me jumpy, distracted, hot. The frequent task of tracking down my wayward cat was all the more daunting because of the audience it prompted. It was challenging always being scrutinized.

"Sundia! Where did you go this time?!" I felt even more foolish than normal searching for my cat. Most Togolese acquaintances did not share a fondness for pets and they would never have tried to contain one in a small living space. Dogs and cats were on their own, roaming in packs at nighttime or engaging in noisy fights. I was a double curiosity: looking and behaving so oddly chasing a cat.

Once in public for routine tasks, there were people to greet in one, two, or three languages. I had to remember to address men differently from women and to distinguish elders from peers. I remembered to ask about their families, extend my right hand, even if it meant shifting three market bags. In addition to the linguistic and cultural challenges, there were physical obstacles in venturing outside. Deep pits in roads or pathways threatened to sprain my weak ankles. How embarrassing it would be to trip in front of everyone! There were often speeding motorcycles to dodge, putrid billows of truck exhaust to circumnavigate. And often I met small groups of over-friendly men. They'd sing out a chorus of cheerful hellos:

"Ça va?"

"Eh! Mah-dahm MAY-ra-deet!"

"BonJOUR Mees Pike!"

I replied with a round of handshakes and a shy smile. I was beginning to remember names, linking Jean Baptiste to his penchant for wearing colorful bellbottoms, associating Philippe with his swagger and keeping track of other people by way of accents, eyebrows, and *gris-gris* necklaces, worn by men and women to keep evil away. At the beginning, the constant social rituals were exhausting. Some evenings when alone, I resolved to stay home and eat boiled ignams and tomato sauce for the third day in a row, thinking wearily about the courage, the patience, the social finesse it took to venture out and buy ingredients for a different meal. I prioritized private time over the lure of fresh eggs (available only on certain days), skewers of grilled chicken sold out by noon at Chez Herbert, and miniature bananas, sweet and pulpy. More often I chose to stay home and enjoy the peace. The adventures of heading out to do errands had become so cumbersome and time-consuming. I supposed I was getting used to life in Lama-Kara when it wasn't so much fun anymore and took it as a positive sign of adjustment.

Beyond the social demands of my larger community, there was the adjustment to living in a compound. The constant noises of children playing and running about, babies crying, adults bickering or laughing or shouting greetings as their friends passed was my auditory backdrop. Added to that were vehicles coughing, screeching, groaning. There was very little silence in my world. And even when I didn't venture out and chose to stay home, my time was not necessarily my own. I tried to be a good sport about sharing my time, my space and my few possessions with neighbors and new friends. Children from the compound and sometimes adults from not-so-distant villages appeared at my doorstep unannounced, any day, any time. Sometimes they stood outside, clapped an "I-am-here; are you there?" rhythm to announce the visit, and waited for me to usher them inside. More often, people just walked up my steps and through my new screen doors, plopping themselves on the large, dusty cushions in my living room. They sat, curious and cheerful, waiting for me to offer them something to drink or eat and join them in lively conversation.

"*Ah, bonjour Miss!* This is my nephew Mori. Your house looks nice now. New furniture, no?"

"Oh, hi Evangeline!" I called from the kitchen finishing up a fresh batch of boiled and filtered water. "I'll be right there."

"What do you think of the freshly graded road?" Placing the cover on the heavy ceramic filter, I wiped my hands and walked into the living room. I was hoping to correct some student work and write some letters home that morning, but those tasks would have to wait. I was happy at first with all the company, but the unpredictability of visits, their endless duration and my increasing inability to control how I spent my time became frustrating, and I began to close my crooked wooden doors and explain to my compound mates that I needed uninterrupted time to work. I'd never thought of myself as a particularly private person.

"I'm going to do some work now!" I'd call to neighbors. "Can you please tell visitors I have much to do for school?"

I felt like a curmudgeon when I closed the doors or asked people to leave. I'd always felt confused about time alone. I planned for it, coveted it, protected it, but only in limited doses. I mostly preferred to be with people. Togolese did nearly everything with others. No one ate or slept or walked or worked alone. People were always together. Privacy was not a cultural value and I was quickly learning how challenging it was to try to claim it.

"Evangeline and Mori, I have to do some work now," I finally figured out a polite way to ask them to leave. It had been nearly three hours.

"Work?? Now?? This is not a work day!" they called out in unison. I envied the other Americans who could more easily spend uncounted hours with their Togolese acquaintances and I tried to imagine their unscheduled lives. But from an early age I had been busy, my happiness dependent on my productivity. I blamed it on the work I had to do as a teacher. But honestly, I was the one who created those to-do lists: lessons to prepare, quizzes to correct, letters to write. And I wanted to keep up with my reading: the folded and fondled Time Magazine (read already many times in transit) that arrived about a month late, not to mention the books I'd brought along or borrowed. These were the books from my last year in college. I'd already finished *My Antonia, Lady Chatterley's Lover, The Heart is a Lonely Hunter, and Passage to India.* But *The Magus, Anna Karenina* and *Ishi* tantalized me from my stack of next reads at the top my new bookshelf. The constant gaze of strangers, the endless visits, the many mysterious rules had me aching for more time to myself.

Nonetheless, our shared shower had worked out well and I seemed to have no trouble taking turns with a dozen others. The common latrine was a different story. It came to embody my discomfort with communal living. As in all compounds, it was situated as far as possible from the living area, strategically set away from the row of rooms, the sheltered cooking area, and the open space where people squatted and ate together or where kids studied by the faint light of candles or kerosene lamps late into the night. When the latrine was constructed for our compound, maybe ten years before, builders met rocks just below the soil surface. They were impenetrable, impervious, impossible to break. With no other option but to build the latrine on the rock bed, builders went up. Up and up and up. The latrine sat on a system of steps that ascended high above the millet stalks, high above the corrugated metal roof of the marketplace, like a lookout tower over the town. Except, of course, that the latrine had to be enclosed, so a potentially lovely view was stifled by 15-foot iron walls. The metal box was humid, clammy most of the year, full of creeping, crawling, flying insects and home to a blend of unpleasant odors. In spite of its detractions, the latrine was distinctive because of its height and location. Everyone I ran into knew about it. They called it The Throne.

"You live in the compound with The Throne?" people asked with both envy and compassion.

"My latrine? You know about it?" I replied curiously, wondering how people from other towns had learned this. I lived near an unsuspecting landmark.

My attitude and good humor about the latrine changed when the season changed. During the short and long rains, slender green poles of millet were my fence, my shade, my moat. I was comforted by the protection the leafy stalks provided. So visiting The Throne during the rainy season wasn't so bad. I'd wind unobserved down a narrow path through the millet stalks. It was even scenic. Once at The Throne, I'd knock to make sure it was vacant, open the heavy metal door, climb the steps and become dubious royalty for a short time, toilet paper in hand.

But at the end of the rainy season, as the dry season gradually sucked moisture from grasses, plants and poles, the millet forest disappeared. The stalks became brown and brittle, bent and broken, resembling ragged organ pipes. Eventually, the canes withered and my forest became a scruffy field. During this season, my lack of privacy was intensified. I couldn't visit the latrine without being tracked by anyone within an observable distance: people out for a casual walk, the throngs of shoppers on Market Day, vendors, children, even my students passing through the heart of town. Privacy? Not a chance.

For this reason, I dreaded getting sick. And although my digestive system was hardy, I had the inevitable encounters with upset stomachs. In fact, I'd had minor issues with food, weather, insects several times already. Bouts of dysentery were excruciating for more reasons than the stomach cramps. My neighbors, now familiar with my daily rhythm, sent kids to me with a bowl of porridge, a bunch of bananas and some suspicious-smelling tea. They'd witnessed my fourth, or fifth trip to The Throne in an hour, more wobbly and weakened than the four previous trips, playing to a sell-out crowd each time. No number of bananas or servings of rice helped to prevent yet another semi-delirious stagger to The Throne.

My compound mates who also used The Throne never seemed to have the same problems, social or physical, that tormented me. They never seemed to get sick. How was that possible? Why was my system so sensitive? I determined to stop eating so much spicy food. I was happy for my Togolese neighbors but as for me, I just couldn't get used to the most private of acts becoming public. I ached for greater privacy. My goal at the outset, to "become African in Africa" was proving so much more difficult than I'd imagined.

> The rhythm was impossible to miss, flowing from the hips to shift
> my legs right and left along with everybody else's, as organic as a
> long breath divided into beats; we almost didn't need the drum.
>
> —**EILEEN DREW**, *The Ivory Crocodile*

AFRICAN BOYFRIENDS

MEN APPEARED EVERYWHERE. Teachers, trainers, culture experts, language consultants, directors, doctors, drivers, sweepers, idlers, vendors, tour guides. They were all ages, married, single, somewhere between, mostly West African and always friendly. Gosh, so many men. So unlike the few unavailable Americans I'd encountered in college. Those young men had been so disinterested, preoccupied with their studies, other girls or political movements. The one young man who

With early friends, Daniel and André

had been off-and-on interested, the fellow I ended up marrying for a brief time, turned out to be a much better candidate as a boyfriend than as a compatible husband. I came to discover that a long courtship did not get better with marriage, to our parents' great vexation. Now, so many miles from our Berkeley struggles, I was single, free and relieved. I agreed with several close friends that now, finally, my life was at a new beginning. The opportunity to live and work in Africa was proof.

Happy to be single, men and dating were not a priority as I relocated to Togo. As if to test my resolve, my first encounter with African trainers in Canada and then in Togo presented an abundance of opportunities to meet single men. Forces pulled me in opposite directions. Eager to be free and independent, I also yearned for company, and romantic company was new and enticing. Finally settled in my home in Lama-Kara and preoccupied with teaching, I learned that the Mr. Perfect I'd fallen hard for in Quebec and longed for in Lomé was already dating someone else in his country far away. I was crushed. I reminded myself of everything that'd attracted me to him. He was stunningly handsome. He was discreet, having kept our alliance secret, at least as far as I knew. He was smart, having navigated the cultural hurdles that international study required. He was caring and affectionate and devoted to his large sprawling family back home. And he was a happy distraction during the grueling days of training. He was so perfect. I channeled my regret at his lack of long term commitment into lesson prep, trying to convince myself that I was too busy to think about boyfriends anyway. But my heart ached for the life I wouldn't have with Mr. Perfect.

Lama-Kara presented a new wave of charmers. I learned that relationships with men in Togo were direct, straightforward, transparent.

Where before I'd met indifference, here I was beautiful. My ready smile, I was beginning to realize, was not only permission for my students to chatter, it was also a magnet for admiring men.

"Far out!" I wrote to my best friend at home. "Handsome men are everywhere!" Victor, Djabarou, Dieudonné, and Patrice swirled around me offering French lessons, peanut candy rolls or sugary *beignets,* still warm, available from the nearby street vendor. On another day they wanted to accompany me to the section of the market where I could find the best lemons. I remembered Maurice, Moussa, and Koffi from Lomé who took me to the beach where they pointed out areas to avoid because of broken glass, raw sewage, roaming gangs.

"Don't go over there," they'd advised. "Those fellows are from Nigeria. They'll steal your watch, grab your bag and pretend to be selling you something." I listened attentively and decided to do what they counseled, uncharacteristically placing caution before adventure, careful to believe that not all Nigerians were bandits.

Men I encountered in Lama-Kara were even more eager to be helpful. They were the same way with local women. It wasn't just because I was American, smiled easily or lived in the center of town. Possessive and paternal these men were, doing their best to make sure I didn't get sick, injured, cheated, or robbed. They wove their way into conversations so easily and were so polite. They laughed so readily. They were so interested in me! I was dazzled.

My first African boyfriend back home had been a sort of orientation course, so I was not completely naïve about the flirtatious attention coming at me in Togo. I'd met Isaac from Ghana in San Francisco when he was a business student working part-time as a Peace Corps recruiter.

He relished having me as a captive audience and gave long lectures on African independence movements, or told elaborate tales about his heroes, Kwame Nkrumah and Julius Nyerere who were paving the way for their people's autonomy and self-governance. Often, in the middle of a monologue, he'd bleat out a loud high-pitched laugh or he'd stop talking altogether, and peer wistfully beyond me. Ten years after Ghanaian independence, he had big dreams for his country and ambitious goals for himself. He was so confident and hard-working, I was certain he'd achieve just about anything he set out to do. He was also sexy and passionate and introduced me to physical pleasure.

"Walk across the room for me," he would say. "I want to see your beautiful hips move." Beautiful hips? I was used to being admired for being strong and sporty, not shapely or alluring. Isaac lowered his deep voice and took long, deliberate pauses moving between words that swung from historic to erotic. Self-consciously I played along as he spoke of making love in strange places (bathtubs) surrounded by provocative scents (patchouli, musk). His deliberate manner of speech elevated what had always seemed seedy. Isaac's self-importance and dignity made everything he did appear the act of a chief. When Peace Corps delayed on my application, Isaac threatened to quit. I watched and waited and he applied pressure.

"Does my recommendation mean nothing?" he'd boomed to colleagues in the San Francisco Peace Corps office, pitting his value as a recruiter against the endless bureaucratic obstacles of a sprawling agency. His ultimatum worked; his confidence swelled. Unsure of whether or not this was Isaac's doing, I lucked out. Peace Corps not only accepted me, but offered me my first choice of destinations: Francophone (French-speaking) Africa. I'd requested Togo because it was adjacent to Isaac's country. I figured having his family two days' travel away would be helpful if a mishap occurred. So even though I was not completely innocent about the flirtatious ways of African men, thanks to Isaac, and even though I was happy being single in Lama-Kara, there were moments when I questioned my solitude. Living alone so far from home, seeking connections and being immersed in a social, sexy culture pointed me in the direction of an African sweetheart.

Michel, the regional pharmacist, was the first to appear in my early days in Lama-Kara. He spoke fluent English, knew many antidotes for mysterious tropical ailments, and circulated in a vast network of influential friends.

"Tell your mother to stay off her swollen foot," he said to the local judge when we met him one afternoon while walking through town. "She needs to give her ankle time to heal. Give her this to reduce the swelling." He reached into his pocket and handed the man some tablets. How did he know we'd run into him? Michel was always available, generous, perceptive and kind. He'd completed his studies at a large American university in the Midwest and upon returning to Togo, was sent north by the government. I thought that was an unfortunate waste of his skills. His linguistic and cross-cultural insights would've been so much more useful in the cosmopolitan region of the capital city. Stuck in the north, he found himself catering to villagers who were more comfortable with the traditional healer than with the town pharmacist. By default, Michel became the intermediary between the locals and far-flung Americans who found themselves in trouble.

I regretted not being more attracted to Michel, for he would have made a wonderful boyfriend. He was smart, sweet, and honest. He tried convincing me that he was the guy for me by visiting frequently when I first arrived, making arrangements to have more furniture built, buying choice cuts of beef at the market, or delivering French cheese and German beer he'd brought up from Lomé. In short, Michel made everything easier. I was grateful for his generous attention but ultimately was drawn to a more mysterious type.

Like a suitor lining up with the golden slipper, Laméga arrived next. Not mysterious at all, he was effusive, loud and happy and fast, and his irrepressible cheerfulness attracted me. He lacked all self-consciousness, draping himself over his pals as he spoke, shouting greetings, noisier than the trucks roaring past.

"AHHAH! HALO!" He dominated conversations, laughing, jabbing, slapping bystanders and often spitting or slobbering as he spoke because his mouth couldn't keep up with his exclamations.

"Halo! *Mais vous aussi! VOUS-LA?!!*" He tossed a bouquet of hellos to everyone around him, from the *chef du village* to local merchants to the group of French teachers and engineers who lived in their own compound on the other side of town. His echoing laughter and generous good nature pulled people toward him. Before I could catch up, he was organizing dinner-dance parties at my place. About a dozen of us would gather and eat *fufu* (pounded ignam) and peanut stew. We rearranged my living room to be a social hall and sat in chairs and on pillows lining the perimeter. Then we danced for hours to the reggae beat of Jimmy Cliff or the highlife tunes of African Brothers International. Laméga was the self-appointed MC, changing tapes, calling out song titles or artists, and pulling the non-dancers out of their chairs and off their cushions to join the rest of us. Shirt open and pants practically falling off, he always appeared slightly undressed, like he'd stopped midway in his belting and buttoning. Shirttails flying and shoes flopping and sliding, Laméga took up lots of space on the dance floor, much like his voice did in conversation. He was fluid on his feet and it was exhilarating to be an extension of his smooth and expansive rhythmic holds and releases.

"Look at those two!" Our friends would pause to watch as our highlife shuffles and hip swings moved in synchrony. We wove in and out of pulls and gentle tosses, always swiveling our hips to the steady beat of the music. The necessary focus and physical harmony were intoxicating. As Laméga's partner, I forgot about the heat, danced off all the weight I'd gained from *beignets*, and managed to momentarily escape the pressure of lesson plans. But eventually, when the music stopped and we walked away from each other and the dancing, I found myself retreating protectively from his forceful style. His tendency to take over with little regard for me or anyone else made me slightly resentful and impatient.

"I've organized a party for Thursday night," he told me one morning. "We'll meet *chez toi* at 7:30. My sister's family will join us and if you make a big stew, she'll bring ignams."

"Thursday? Tomorrow? I have to prepare tests for three classes. I can't possibly have a party," I said, feeling like an invisible piece in Laméga's social quilt. "*J'ai trop de travail*," I told him, prioritizing my work over his good-natured organizing. When the "*trop de travail*" reply popped up more and more frequently, his visits tapered off. I wanted to be more direct with him, but Laméga was well-intentioned and too kind-hearted for me to say outright that he was just not the guy for me.

While I worked slowly at discouraging Laméga, Koffi, my carpenter, was stepping up his courting behavior. These sleek, cheerful men reminded me of plumed birds, each taking a turn strutting ahead of the pack. Koffi could've been a model. Strikingly attractive with refined wooing skills, his shoulder curves seemed to mimic the smooth corner curve of the desk he was crafting for me. Perhaps my questionable perception was influenced by the malaria medication I was taking, the continuous attention from men, my utter naïvete, the nonstop socializing and lack of private time to pause and reflect. Suddenly his arm was around my waist.

"Oh!" I gasped. His fine woodworking skills, willingness to customize any furniture request to my odd specifications (two large holes in this narrow table to accommodate enameled bowls?!) and the repeated winks he directed my way did not outweigh the five years between us. Young men seemed old. Misperceptions notwithstanding, I was not swayed by his solicitations.

And then André appeared. He was different. Shorter than Laméga with a more demure public presence, he was definitely more mysterious than Michel. He had a sweet smile, kind brown eyes and a soft voice. André was a *policier*. I'd never been drawn to men in uniforms (perhaps repelled is more accurate for someone emerging from the Civil Rights struggle and the anti-war movement), so I found it curious to be smitten by a gentle man in khaki. The perfect creases, the sharp shoulder lines, the tight fit of his uniform showcased André's short strong body and his beautiful round face. His mild manner and calm style contrasted with the stereotype I'd harbored of American policemen. We met for the first time in the compound of a local seamstress, the two of us wanting to commission clothes that reflected our new roles. I entered a corner of the sewing studio strewn with shirts and pants and gowns and stretches of fabric as André and the seamstress were talking.

"Phew!" I exclaimed, walking in on André and Madame Tchassi, breathing hard and perspiring from the dry, hot weather. *"Vous êtes la couturière, n'est-ce pas?"* I inadvertently interrupted them, making sure I was in the right place. Stepping aside, André welcomed me and invited me to make my requests, pausing in the middle of his.

"Oui, Mademoiselle, vous êtes chez la couturière ici. Soyez la bienvenue! Est-ce que je peux vous aider a commander quelques vêtements?' He asked if he could assist me in ordering the dresses I needed. How gracious and polite he was. He waited while Madame Tchassi took my measurements, examined the brightly colored fabric I'd brought and listened carefully to my curious requests: round-collared, buttoned-opening, sleeveless dress, short, about halfway between my knees and my waist.

"Pas trop courte, Mademoiselle??!" Madame kept asking. She'd never ever made a dress so short. André turned to her suggesting she make the hem extra long so that if I decided the dress was too short it could be easily lengthened. How clever and helpful he was. He didn't resume his order with the seamstress until I began walking away, happily distracted as I imagined standing in front of my students in my brand new African-cloth mini-dress. I'd already sewn two dresses from hand, but no longer had extra time, even if I used the sewing machine at school, so coming upon a seamstress was a fun and practical option. I'd never worn custom-made clothes.

Like me, André was new to this part of Togo, assigned to the north after school and police training. We passed each other several times in the next few weeks doing errands around town. His tentativeness was such a contrast to Michel's over-preparedness, Laméga's need to control and Koffi's over-confidence. I wasn't overwhelmed by André. His polite,

André in **uniform**

timid approach made him immensely appealing, so I invited him to visit me at my compound. More courteous than he needed to be, he kept his visits short and infrequent. As we learned about each other's families, jobs and musical tastes, we became friends. This was the first time André had lived in the north and he missed his family desperately, particularly his grandma, Mamavie. I practiced saying her name and envied his close relationship with his grandmother. André loved highlife music and promised to introduce me to his favorite musicians. Fela? Bella Bellow? People were crazy about musicians I'd never heard of. I loved the music and was eager to learn about it. We also made plans to get to know the region.

With a few friends, André and I took motor-scooter rides to nearby villages around Lama-Kara. We visited a market and the village of another Peace Corps volunteer together. I had a new Peace Corps-issued mobylette, purchased for volunteers living in areas that were far away or hilly. They were gearless, motorized one-speed bicycles with accelerators, brakes, lights and horns that bleated like sad sheep. They were fun to drive and status symbols to most of my Togolese acquaintances.

André and I were relieved to have each other as friends in our new surroundings. We kept each other company on rare shared days off and practiced new dance steps, since we always listened to music. He taught me how to wiggle my hips without moving my shoulders and how to follow a gentleman's lead. Like this, so innocently, I warmed up to his touch and moved into his tender hold. Little by little and over many weeks, we peeled away the layers of curiosity, shyness and caution, and became lovers. Peace Corps had counseled us repeatedly about the importance of birth control, including what we requested in our well-stocked clinic-in-a-box medical kits. Many volunteers had Togolese sweethearts. Many others chose fellow volunteers as boy- or girlfriends. It seemed quite natural to have a lover and everyone was accepting, locals and foreigners, even encouraging of romantic relationships.

In letters home I announced that I'd met the man of my dreams. "The REAL THING!" I announced to my girlfriends who had heard me exclaim this several times before. "No, really! He's perfect!" And through exuberant reports home, through the many hours of waiting, anticipating his visits, through my isolation and eagerness to feel settled and to justify this all in some greater long-term purpose, I fantasized a future with this beautiful young man. I'd take him home with me at the end of two years, show him around my childhood neighborhood, introduce him to former colleagues, charm my mother, father and stepmother with his polite manners, and present the gifts he'd bring to each of them. I made it clear to other suitors that André was my African boyfriend and to my great relief, the parade of eager men subsided. André and I were so compatible. Being sweethearts with him was a lovely way to move into my African life. We began to call each other *Bubu* and soon everyone was asking me, *"Comment va Bubu?"* How's Bubu?!

"Pttt-t-t-t." From my small kitchen, I heard the soft steady coughs of André's aquamarine Vespa and ran out to meet him when he came to visit. Still straddling the motorcycle, he skillfully maneuvered around the wavy tin walls of the compound cooking area, edging the scooter into the space between my front steps and the tiny flower garden.

"*Bonjour!!*"

"*Monsieur le Policier est arrivé!*"

"*Waow!*" Children from the compound came running towards him, shouting as he arrived. He stepped off, set the kickstand, removed his helmet and reached into his pocket, handing pennies or peanuts to each of the kids.

"*Bonjour, mes enfants! Bonjour tout le monde!!*" He called out a musical greeting, passed out treats then shooed everyone away with a big smile. They scattered, skipping and singing, "*Merci, Monsieur Policier! Merci beaucoup!*"

He was here! He was finally here. I tried not to keep track of how late he was.

"*Enfin!*" I always said, wringing my hands on a dishtowel and doing a poor job of concealing my impatience with *l'heure africaine*.

"Africans are never on time," he told me again and again. "We move to a different kind of clock!" All my cultural sensitivity training had not helped me accept chronic tardiness. When he finally came inside, we drank some water, I offered him a piece of one of my latest cakes or cookies, and we caught up on the week.

"The nuns are too mean to the students! The textbooks are so inappropriate!" He listened patiently.

"*Et ta maman? La famille?* Let me say hello to your mother." He insisted on adding a friendly comment to the letter home I was writing. "*Bonjour Madame Pike,*" he wrote in neat cursive at the top of the page. I was no longer annoyed.

Our relationship tiptoed carefully into routines. We spent time together on weekends and often took siestas together during the midday break when businesses closed and schools shut down as no work was possible in the intense heat. Unaccustomed to this three-hour period of inactivity, I laid awake listening to André's gentle breathing and wondered how anyone could be so relaxed to be able to sleep in the middle of the day. He awakened with small beads of sweat on his forehead and upper lip, forced a sleepy smile, turned on the radio and stretched himself into a state of alertness. We showered and dressed and returned to another three hours of work.

In this way, we eased our way into a tender romance. And before long we were a local institution. André met all my acquaintances around town, became famous to my students and was included in all the parties I attended. Polly, with whom I'd been in touch regularly, found it awkward accompanying us everywhere, so we introduced her to André's friend Daniel who became Polly's boyfriend. I was so proud of her willingness to accept what I'd come to consider an uplifting element of life: romance. She seemed happier. The four of us now took excursions together, continuing to explore new parts of the country, meeting people from different regions who introduced us to more new languages and local crafts. We returned home from these escapades with grass mats, clay pots, metal figurines. André always bought something for Mamavie. Polly and I were happy and unself-conscious about our attachments. Romance was natural here, encouraged, expected. It was a jubilant period of growing intimacy, friendship and discovery.

Music swiftly became a significant part of my life, constantly playing on the radio, blaring from others' cassette recorders, featured at weekend dance concerts and strummed from my guitar. I tried to learn something different, either chord progressions or finger configurations or new songs, every day. The compound kids loved what I played and listened awestruck. I'd performed "Row, Row, Row Your Boat" and "Michael Row the Boat Ashore" to their euphoric applause. When André visited, we tried to catch Radio Lomé Pop Music Roundup in the early evening. The program played local music straight for two hours. Then we danced to highlife, bebop and reggae. It was enchanting. When we weren't dancing or eating or chatting with my compound neighbors, André took me by the police station and we chatted with the fellows on duty. They sure didn't seem to have much work. They just sat and welcomed a steady stream of passers-by. I finally understood that a visit to the police station gave André an excuse to avoid using The Throne. He avoided my latrine. Unfortunately, I didn't have another option.

André's visits always ended too soon. He climbed back on his Vespa, maneuvered it out of its parking spot and handed one of the compound boys some coins for washing the motorcycle.

With André

"*A bientôt, Bubu!*" he called to me and the rest of the compound.

"See you soon!" I replied, hastening inside to finish up some last-minute lesson plans.

MARKET DAY IN LAMA-KARA

" **M**ARCHÉ?!! LAMA-KARA?!! HA-HA-HA!" Fellow volunteers
made fun of my enthusiasm. They considered the Lama-Kara
market mediocre at best. And they had a point, I confessed, when thinking of the more lavish markets in outlying villages and those farther
south. Even so, the market in Lama-Kara was a lifeline to those of us who
lived in and around the town. And to me, especially in the early months,
the market was much more than a source of supplies, so I made sure to
set aside time to attend its regular rollout. Sure, I was able to stock up
on dried and canned tomato paste and replenish household staples like
matches and powdered milk, but there were also surprises like freshly-
roasted peanuts packaged in cones of recycled school notebook paper,
pirated cassette tapes of Jimmy Cliff songs, and maybe a leather trades-
man pedaling crude belts or bags. It wasn't only about merchandise
anyway. For locals, the market was important for connecting with friends
and meeting relatives who came in from nearby villages. For me, market
day offered language lessons, negotiation practice and the experience of
being immersed in a swirl of colors, movement, unforgettable smells and
deafening sounds. Market day was more party than enterprise.

Every sixth day, scores of people filed into town in a well-rehearsed
choreography. From my unwalled compound in the center of the city, I

watched a colorful cavalcade parade toward the large concrete platform from all directions, moving to a common center like tiny ants following one another along the spokes of a bicycle wheel to its hub. People approached the platform, took a giant step up and disappeared under the huge, cascading roof. This expansive metal covering, which people of Kara proudly considered to be evidence of progress, rendered the marketplace an incubator in the dry season, causing everything under it to throb with heat. I tried to make my market visits short but was often pulled into a conversation or left searching for fruit I couldn't find. In the wet season, the roof acted as an amplifier for the rain.

"*Comment va votre famille? La famille?*" the local metalsmith screeched to an acquaintance mid-rainstorm.

"*Marie? C'est qui Marie?*"

"*Non! LA FAMILLE!!*"

The Lama-Kara marketplace

En route to the market

In the rain, no one heard friendly salutations, sales pitches, or older siblings calling their broods. Market-goers (and vendors) shouted all day long and we walked home with headaches. In the weeks between pelting rain and blistering heat, roughly 3-4 months each year, Market Day was fun.

I loved the bright colors, the textures in sound and sight, the festive feeling we all shared anticipating it, experiencing it and recovering from it. How could anyone complain? I awaited fresh tomatoes (rare) or sometimes a mango or two (even more rare.)A highlight for me was

A Collège Adèle student's illustration of a market vendor. "Come and buy things at a good price!"

observing how people dressed. Most wore their very best clothes: women in three-piece outfits of intricate batik patterns in bright greens, blues, oranges. There were Dutch wax fabric prints too, colorful patterns of checkerboards and spider webs, intertwined circles framing portraits of the Togolese president and repeated geometric designs. Some women wore elaborate headdresses, cloth twirled and tied so masterfully that I couldn't imagine how long it took to do this. My friends said it took about two minutes. Wow. Many other women balanced baskets of fruit nestled on crowns of cloth to cushion and level the loads. Some men dressed elegantly, especially those who'd traveled in from the desert. They wore gowns, or *boubous*, and the pastel colors of the polished cloth undulated and changed hue with each long stride. These men often wore turbans or crocheted brimless caps, common for Muslims. Other men, workers, helpers, assistants, mostly men of all ages, wore shorts and nearly always unbuttoned shirts, sweating from the heavy bundles they were transporting in and out of the market. Kids were bent under the weight of their bundles of wood, plastic basins, propane, and bread. Cargo atop their heads freed up their arms to drag chickens, wild turkeys, baskets of baskets and oversized packages of plastics from China. Women sold merchandise, shopped and socialized.

Children darted everywhere, bobbing around their mamas or aunties, boys kicking empty cans back and forth in skillful passes that just missed running dogs, preoccupied villagers and overloaded carts. As they played modified soccer, the boys balanced tin basins or plastic bowls on their heads to hopefully sell or fill. Some dragged great bags of local fabric, firewood, goats or sheep, often cajoling younger brothers or sisters. It was remarkable how hard kids worked and how capable they were. Girls toted younger children on their backs or balanced baskets like the women, or both. On Market Day both boys and girls assumed all the parenting responsibilities that mothers were too busy to perform, keeping the young ones clean, safe, fed, and entertained.

If I wanted meat, I'd have to travel out of town to reserve and purchase a slice of beef. The local butcher would kill a cow at dawn, slice up its various parts and lay them out on a huge rock for display. I hurried to get there before the sun got too hot and the flies set in. The one cow was usually all bought up by 10AM, and those who got there too late had to wait six more days for the next opportunity. So sometimes Market Day entailed an out-of-town adventure.

I walked out my door to go to the market, as always stiffening myself for the encounters ahead, rehearsing the Kabré expressions I had tried to learn. *N'lwalé? Alafia! Kapté! Tononda? N'labalé!* I crossed the dirt road, entered the market and cruised the periphery, scoping out this week's offerings. Men in groups toasted me with morning drinks of the local brew and women called out to have me stop and buy from them.

"*Yovo!* Come here! Buy this!" I approached the third onion vendor, her medium-sized bulbs looking better than those at the other two stands, but she was busy talking to neighbors, the tomato lady and Madame Carved Coconut. Frankly, their businesses seemed much less important than their conversations. I finally broke into their conversation.

N'Iwalé? I asked prices in Kabré, hoping this would earn me a bargain.

Alafia! I forgot to greet them first and shook my head in a nonverbal apology.

Kapté! I replied by welcoming <u>them</u> to the market, hoping this would override my earlier *faux pas*.

Tononda? I followed up with a question about business, hoping further to impress them with my prowess in Kabré. Usually, I was more impressed with my language efforts than anyone else. Unfortunately, these efforts didn't win bargains.

"How much did you ask for the onions?" I signaled to the onion seller in feigned astonishment. "That's impossible! I paid half of that last week for twice as many!" This was true. The older woman, her large buxom body hovered over her table display, where onions were neatly arranged on a tilting cardboard box, looked straight at me and didn't budge on the price. I imagined she must've been annoyed with me for interrupting her conversation with Madame Coconut. Since no one else was selling such impressive onions, I chose not to walk off in a huff to another vendor, so I asked the young man behind me for help. He was speaking a mixture of French and Mina.

"Can you please explain that I live and work in town and that I need onions for a peanut stew I'm making tonight and I teach at Collège Adèle and I'm not a rich diplomat?" I begged him breathlessly.

With a smirk my broker appealed to the onion seller in Kabré. At least that was what I hoped he was doing. He turned to me. "She says the price stays. It cost her eight children and walking all night to get these onions here. She's glad you live here but the price is the same." How could I argue with eight children and half a day's walk? It was uncomfortable challenging the market vendors, especially when I would've gladly paid what they first demanded. But I'd learned that vendors expected to bargain and that shoppers who didn't try to lower prices weren't respected. So I continued to make pitiful attempts to strike a bargain.

Even vendors who recognized me week after week still doubled or tripled their prices when I approached and every purchase required a cumbersome negotiation. Shopping was hard work. The rare batch of bulbous onions weren't the only attraction. I scanned crude hoes, candles, pyramids of dried hot peppers and baskets of ignams. From time to time, I cheered myself up by patronizing the pagne vendor, inspired by the brilliant outfits so many women were wearing, though her cloth selection was quite limited and the quality irregular. When the merchandise was dirty, the prints misaligned or the cotton poorly-woven, I was not tempted to buy. But even then, thumbing through the stacks of neatly-folded fabric offered its own pleasure. I could usually think of reasons to buy another three-meter length. My commissions from the seamstress had turned out well and the new (more professional) dresses she'd made were great for school. They hadn't been expensive, only 400 CFA ($3.50) apiece, so I'd ordered cushion covers too. Over the weeks I gathered fabric for my best friend back home and for my mom. Then I scooted back to the seamstress and requested a skirt, a shirt and a table cover. And there was usually another dress for me! But even with the pagne vendor, the bargaining struggle was onerous.

Though the fruits and vegetables were sometimes shriveled and the textiles in short supply, the Lama-Kara market had a prize. I made my way to a stall at the back of the market by stepping carefully through thick smoke from grilling brochettes, trying not to inhale the odor of rotting vegetables and dried fish, hopping over puddles of filthy water. On lucky days, I'd find the bead seller. He appeared irregularly like the cloth vendor, more absent than not. He and his fellow *Bedouins* came on camel, lugging cloth sacks containing a dizzying variety of African beads. He was Tuareg, impressively tall and graceful, and had traveled across the desert from Agadez or Timbuktu or Ougadougou. I'd never seen anyone like him, dressed in an embroidered gown with long flowing sleeves. His face was narrow, the color of seasoned wood, and his nose was sharp and his chin pointed. His eyes were dark; he rarely looked at me. I didn't greet him because I was intimidated by his seriousness. I felt foolish around him, not knowing the appropriate way to act, but he knew I loved his merchandise.

The beads were strung on heavy straw and wrapped in great, disciplined circles. The smells of dusty burlap, coarse raffia and desert sweat became familiar and pleasant as I fingered the smooth round shapes and fantasized being able to buy them all and plop them into my bag of beads. If I were not careful, much of my weekly allowance of $40.00 would go to buying these treasures. I was relieved the bead-seller didn't come to the market every week. With the broad array of beads, I made *colliers* (necklaces), bracelets, earrings and used them as ornaments for my macramé projects. Bone beads, horn beads and even ivory beads were hidden treasures in the *Tuareg's* bags. Between smoking or drinking tea or talking with friends, he'd push a strand in my direction, indicating with a grunt and a nod that I couldn't leave without buying it. His prices were exorbitant, always, and I was too timid to bargain. He didn't speak any of the languages I'd ventured into and didn't give me the impression his prices would change anyway, so I generally accepted what he proposed. I soon had a small but exquisite collection of African beads.

I knew beads were more than just ornamental. They'd been currency, representations of status and reminders of trade with Europe as far back as the 16th century. And they still signified value. Girls donned beads around their waists when they became women. The colorful strands slung around their hips were sexy and elegant, though they were always concealed under long skirts. Beads and shells decorated drums, calabashes, masks and pieces of furniture. "Venetian" beads, long multi-colored glass beads, were popular among my American friends, although my bead-seller rarely had these. They originated in Venice when European traders began using them as currency nearly 400 years ago. We referred to them as African trade beads.

"*Bubu! Viens voir!*" I called André to show him my most recent acquisition from the day's market purchase.

"*Jolis perles,*" he said, admiring the new beads, rolling a few in his fingers and holding them up to the sunlight.

"*Regardes-ça,*" I commented, handing him some small red cubes and frowning. I pointed out the tiny, tiny holes that weren't string-able, some bead designer's malicious plot to frustrate those of us who wanted to wear our beads. But other types of beads invited my imagination. I wore a strand of African trade beads on my wrist, had a small collection of slender ridged blue beads for a necklace and some round ochre bobbins decorated with green and black dots for my current macramé project. There were simple clay beads and even plastic beads of bright colors. Almost more valuable and certainly more beautiful than money to me, I kept my bead collection wrapped in cloth in a corner of my closet.

As market cycles rolled through to the next season, I wearied of the effort it took to buy and made my market forays shorter, more targeted, and less recreational. I worked from a shopping list and skipped wandering the periphery of the market. With each transaction, whether or not I had been successful at bargaining, I called out *N'labalé*, "Good-bye! Good day!" as I walked away.

The Lama-Kara market introduced me to doing business, meeting vendors and practicing tricky expressions in new languages. I hadn't mastered bargaining and rarely saw my friends there. They continued to dismiss my market, but I could usually track down the most exotic vendor when she or he appeared and I could boast a varied and beautiful bead collection, thanks to a taciturn bead seller whose stash far outshone bead vendors' bags from markets farther south. When Polly, my local friends, and Peace Corps volunteers passing through town noticed the beads in my bracelet or around my neck, they'd start asking questions.

"Where'd you find those?"

"How much did you pay for them?"

"What unusual beads!"

How surprised they were to learn that I'd found such treasures at my local market. They could scoff all they wanted at the lack of mangoes, oranges, and tomatoes, but I remained fiercely loyal to the market in Lama-Kara.

It was January. The rains would not come for several months. When they did come, the thick growth would obscure everything beyond the edge of the road. But for now, the sweep of the land lay bared. I could almost smell the desert lurking, waiting to reclaim the land it had lost to rudimentary vegetation.

—**WENDY LAURA BELCHER**, *Honey from the Lion: An African Journey*

CHANGE OF SEASONS, CHANGE OF SCENE

S INA AND I WERE WALKING the two blocks home from a trip to town where we'd stocked up on bouillon cubes and tomato sauce. My teenage helper, frequent shopping companion and compound "brother" had just bought us sweet warm *beignets*, reminiscent of doughnut holes, loosely packed in a piece of recycled notebook paper. We'd missed market day earlier in the week. A sudden swift wind pushed us from behind

With Sina in Lomé

and blew with it dust, dry leaves and scraps of crumpled paper. My short skirt ballooned with the gust. I tapped it down as Sina quickly pulled our purchases to his chest, protecting them from the grit that swirled in all directions around us. A dramatic change of weather had come our way. We were entering the dry season, three months into my first year and my first experience with the *harmattan*, a wind from the Sahara that billowed and blew throughout the region, bringing tiny particles of silt that found their way into crannies and crevices, indiscriminately dusting every imaginable (and unimaginable) surface. The sand appeared on every tabletop in every room, in my stacks of papers, sprinkled through the pages of books, in hidden cavities of my mobylette, in the folds of my clothes, on my dishes and pots and pans, in my ears, stuck to my bare legs and between my sandaled toes. At noontime we had blasting heat. My sweaty hands stuck to paper, making it challenging to write letters or plan lessons. My short sleeveless dresses did little to keep me comfortable. I revolved in an orbit of sand and sweat. Such fierce midday heat was framed by freezing cold mornings and evenings. No more humidity, no more rain and most regrettably, I could no longer take a morning shower, even when I heated the water. It was just too cold.

This strange, histrionic weather may have been the reason I seemed sick so frequently. As soon as I recovered from one ailment, another came along, a bit like blustering gusts of dust. The recurring stomach-aches, frequent colds, monthly bouts of dysentery challenged my claim to nearly always perfect health. To further undermine my boasts, I jammed a toe into the door and couldn't walk for the throbbing. The toe turned flaming red and swelled, obviously infected, as I hobbled to class in flip-flops. When the toe refused to heal, I tracked down one of the nuns at the school infirmary, submitted to a penicillin shot and almost immediately recovered. But there were also headaches, nausea, weakness. Was it the constantly-changing weather? The food? The malaria medicine? Fumes from the huge trucks? The kerosene lamps? In spite of continual minor health calamities, I never doubted my hardiness. Polly and I had been sent far upcountry because we were strong and resilient, after all. And I'd heard that almost everyone took several months to adjust to such new surroundings.

There was a bright side to the frequent medical mishaps: I got to slow down. And there were pleasant discoveries when I set aside my regular hectic schedule. Three of the nuns came to visit when I was under the weather. I didn't think they ever left the school. I showed them around my place, introduced them to my kitty and pointed out my latrine. They had a good laugh at The Throne. I was happy and surprised to see a less severe side to my ultra-serious colleagues.

André, too, was attentive as I passed from one health challenge to another. He visited frequently and brought with him chicken brochettes, peanuts or Coke. I adored him more each time I got sick. Happily, the other suitors (all looking for American wives, I was told) kept their distance. I'd made it clear that André was my only boyfriend. Although André and I had pledged to be "exclusive," I was following my own advice and trying to keep the relationship lighthearted, although this wasn't so easy for me. A recent conversation convinced me that he saw our relationship as temporary.

"*Comment*?!" I asked about something he'd said, not sure of what he meant. "You're going to <u>what</u> six months after I leave Togo?"

"*Je vais me marier!*" he replied matter-of-factly.

"You're getting married?!" I was aghast.

He planned to marry six months after I went home. He calculated carefully. I'd leave in two years, when he turned 24. He wanted his future children to support him by the time he turned 50. What a strange, deliberate way to plan something that's impossible to schedule. Didn't you wait to marry until after you fell in love? I wondered whether to applaud his practicality or be disturbed by his lack of long-term commitment. For now my hope was that in two years we'd be so attached to each other that he wouldn't want to live without me.

These days we were spending more time together. Mostly we listened to the radio but when I was feeling fine and we both had a free evening, we went to the local cinema. The "theater" was really an open, airy room with wooden benches and a huge white screen. The films, so far only Westerns or war dramas, were powered by a generator that bolted and shimmied depending on its supply of water-powered electricity. When the power ran low, the movie lumbered to a near-stop and everyone started yelling.

"*Eh!*" one man stood up and shouted.

"*Le film s'accroche!*" Another bellowed that the film was stuck.

"*Vous les autorités! Faites quelque chose!!!*" A third demanded that the technicians do something. Cinema staff ran to the rescue, furiously pumping water to get things going again. The film grabbed momentum and viewers quieted down. As for the movies, I was fascinated by the superhuman caprices of film heroes, but the audience was much more entertaining. People cheered or booed the entire length of the film.

"*Hurrah! Oui! Comme ça!*"

"*Non, non, non! Arretez!*"

What also caught my attention were the scenes of green grass, lush meadows, the sea, modern flashy cars and hip Western clothes. The once familiar images seemed strange and far away. This must've been a sign that I was becoming more comfortable where I was. The weather was bizarre but *c'est vrai que je m'y habitue*. For westerners, it seemed more and more true that Africa was a question of familiarity and I was really settling in. Peace Corps wanted us to be healthy and feel comfortable so that our work and community roles would be effective.

Finally accustomed to my immediate neighborhood, I was eager to get out and explore the greater region on weekends. So when we could, Polly came up from Sokodé, and she, André and I escaped the noise, heat and wind in town to visit a nearby village. The surrounding fields, lush with young plants, were a refreshing contrast to the barren open spaces in town. On one of these ventures we met a young boy who stopped and offered to make each of us personalized name stamps. We were game and watched as he scribbled our names and affiliations on a much-used notebook page.

Image from my hand-carved name stamp

Then, razorblade in hand, he proceeded to deftly carve what he'd written onto small wooden blocks. We delighted in the results and took the new "identity stamps" as validation that each of us was in the right place doing just the right thing. Mine said MEREDITH PIKE * COLLEGE ADELE * LAMA-KARA * TOGO *AF *. We pocketed our seals, paid our inventive entrepreneur and continued on our way a bit more gleefully. I used water color paint on my oval-shaped name stamp and printed it on most every book, letter, lesson plan and postcard.

Going out on adventures was only possible when I was caught up with schoolwork. I loved the challenge of designing good lessons but the workload continued to be insurmountable. And worse, when there were lulls in my weekly race to prep, correct and teach, I doubted my effectiveness. I wondered if I ever actually taught anything. And if I had, would my students ever use what they'd learned? If not, why was I working so hard? When these questions got me down, I tried something new in the classroom, a new game or a new song. I taught students "Itsy-Bitsy Spider" one week and "I'm a Little Teapot" the next.

"*Teapot, Mees, Teapot?*" they begged me to practice singing during a lull in the lesson.

"Do your homework tonight, everyone, and we'll start tomorrow with a song," I bribed. It was hard to stay discouraged. And though it didn't feel so much like Christmas with hot, hot days, we were into the holiday season and we celebrated with Christmas music and modest gifts. I played my guitar until my fingers had blisters. Students exchanged beautiful handmade cards and we all ate cookies. The festivities distracted me from my worries about teaching effectiveness.

There were additional distractions in curious scenes around town.

On our errands together, Sina helped me understand.

"*Pourquoi ca?*" I asked when I saw a large group of people waving sticks and running after a man in scruffy clothes. "Why are they screaming and chasing him?"

"*C'est un voleur.*" He was a thief, a robber.

"*Tu le connais? Tu l'as vu déjà? Comment tu sais?*" I asked more questions and learned that Sina didn't know him, hadn't seen him before. This was what happened when people stole. They were chased and beaten. I turned away from the savage scene, citizens taking the law into their own hands. I stepped up my pace, hoping to escape either witnessing or hearing how villagers punished the suspect.

On another day I saw what had become an unpleasantly familiar scene, a trio of skinny, hungry dogs rifling through a heap of garbage for something edible. I asked Sina why everyone hated dogs.

"*Ils sont sales. Ils passent des maladies. Ils mangent des poules.*" He told me that they were dirty, they spread disease, they ate chickens. I hated how mean people were with animals. I got sick to my stomach each time I saw people kicking dogs or scaring cats away. This cultural difference was tough for me.

Sina clarified some other cultural differences.

"Why can't I use my red pen to write letters? Why can't I sing when I eat? Or practice songs in the shower?" According to him, people only wrote in red when someone had died. And singing in the shower was definitely not good.

"*Ce n'est pas bon!*" he asserted. I guessed it had come from a superstition, and I was wise to respect such deep-rooted beliefs.

Sina's lessons saved me from making big mistakes. I listened to him and followed his advice. And every once in a while I remembered Denis and the similar role he had played as informant when I'd first arrived in Quebec. I so depended on my young pals. Still no letter from Denis.

When I wasn't feeling up to it, Sina did errands for me and brought me beans and rice, *patte* and sauce, or whatever the family was eating. On shopping trips, we bought roasted peanuts or warm sugar-coated beignets and brought them home to the kids in the compound. To show Sina how much I appreciated his loyal assistance, I invited him to accompany me to Lomé during winter vacation.

"*C'est vrai?*" He asked me to repeat what I'd said with wide eyes and a trembling smirk, not sure he'd heard right but unable to contain his delight if he had. Sina had never been outside Lama-Kara. He'd never taken a train, visited a city, seen the ocean. I'd never made the trip south on my own, so André's brother agreed to travel with us and help navigate the transfers and delays, for there were bound to be delays. We secured permission from Sina's uncle and my landlord to head south for a brief visit. The entire compound mobilized to send us off.

We rose at 3AM to make our way to the station for a 5AM bus. We'd planned to take a bus to the train station, and then go all the way to Lomé by train. When we arrived nearly two hours early at the large field that doubled as terminal, there were two buses waiting but no more seats on either bus. Both were filled with students leaving for Christmas vacation. I wondered why I hadn't predicted this. Exercising supreme flexibility, we hopped on a small truck and were on our way south by 4AM. I figured an early departure would mean an early arrival. We arrived at the train station and met huge noisy crowds. Thank goodness I had someone to tell me what to do. People pushed and yelled. I panicked momentarily, observing that no one formed a line. What if I got separated from Sina?

Lost my way? Was pushed in the wrong direction? I linked arms with Sina and grabbed André's brother's elbow, walking as a threesome to the correct platform to board the train for Lomé. We dodged others who got on with live chickens, tethered goats, six-foot stacks of basins, bursting suitcases and lots of noise and confusion. Confusion for me, anyway. There was laughter, friendly greetings, and generous moving about to let others pass. Sina took this all in stride.

"*C'est quoi, ça?*" he asked with alarm as the train finally departed.

"Oh, that's the sound of the train!" I said. The confusion was familiar to him, but the crunching, grinding, squeaking sounds of the locomotive were entirely new.

We were on our way, making frequent stops on our way south. I'd known there were stops, but didn't realize there were so many. At each station, vendors mobbed the open train windows offering us oversized ignams, dark bottles of alcohol, baskets, brochettes. Passengers ate as we proceeded slowly south, sampling different agricultural regions along the way. Products from the south became available as the vistas changed from muted green trees and beige fields to dark green trees and red earth. In the south now, palm oil, pineapples and long, shiny poles of sugar cane became available. The train ride was long, we were exhausted, but we never complained. It was all new and lively and colorful at this festive, happy time of year.

"*Ça fait trente-six!*" Sina announced as we arrived at the thirty-sixth stop, pulling into the Lomé train station. Thirty-six stops, 380 kilometers and 236 miles in six and a half hours! In spite of feeling exhausted and in need of showers, we were exhilarated to get to the big city.

"*Enfin!* Finally!" we chorused, looking at each other and laughing.

In Lomé, we settled in at Edith's Inn. By then I knew what to expect and was eager for some familiar city comfort. Having lived so simply for three months in Lama-Kara, I resurfaced appreciative of what Edith's Inn offered. I supposed Edith had been right, I conceded. Her prediction that I'd be a changed person upon my return to Lomé was correct, or at least I hoped so. I was happier and more self-assured than I'd been three months earlier and welcomed the role of guide for twelve-year-old Sina. Once settled, we spent most of each day walking around town, taking in the traffic, the noise of cars, trucks, motorcycles, the line of palm trees along the coast and the changing tide levels at the beach.

"*Mees*," Sina confessed. "*Je n'ai jamais vu choses comme ça*." He'd never seen anything like these sights, the neighborhoods of two-story buildings, the tall hotels, the noisy clusters of men and children in the streets

The beach in Lomé

dodging honking cars and beeping motorcycles. He stuck close to me, mostly silent, awaiting the next urban spectacle.

We got invited to dinner at friends' homes and even went swimming at a hotel pool. Everyone was so kind to Sina, applauding him for his worldly interests and commending him on his courage to be so far away from home so young. He'd probably never spent so much time away from siblings, cousins or friends. I wondered if he was lonely. It was a busy, gutsy week for both of us and I felt happy for once showing Sina the way. We ventured west across the border to Ghana to send Christmas packages to my friends and family members in the States, and spent several hours in the vast and well-known Lomé market to buy fabric, mangoes and bananas.

"*Tout est très, très bon.*" Sina appreciated all the new sights and experiences, the meals with my American friends, his first visit to a "big" city. "*Mais Lama-Kara me manque!*" He was homesick for Lama-Kara. Aha! I suspected so.

"*Moi aussi, Sina!*" I shared his eagerness to go back. At the end of six days, we were both ready to return to our small town where everything was familiar, where life seemed way more manageable. We caught a crowded *Peugeot* "taxi" and with a swift ride north, returned to a compound crowd of revelers, all the kids and some neighbors cheering and dancing for our arrival and for Christmas.

Christmas fell on Market Day, so it was a double celebration. Everyone attended Mass on Christmas Eve, and then feasted on meat, goat or chicken stew—a special treat. On Christmas day we joined the parade around the marketplace in bright new outfits. I surprised Sina with an outfit I'd commissioned and André surprised me with a new dress that matched an outfit of his! Even the kids wore new clothes and those who hadn't gotten something new were striking in clean school uniforms. The local radio station played reggae or Afrobeat versions of Christmas carols and we spent the afternoon dancing. Festive local music was everywhere, high-pitched flute spiraling around drum rhythms. But Christmas in the heat was not at all familiar and an itty-bitty pit in my stomach (homesickness? nostalgia?) tiptoed in and out of my consciousness.

Sudden free time caught me by surprise. With school vacation, André's excessive work schedule, and no letters from friends or family for weeks, I fought off a longing for home by busying myself with sewing projects and cooking. Then New Year's Eve arrived. My sadness at being so far away from family and the crazy feeling of Christmas in the summertime welled up behind my eyes and I spent most of the day in tears. André wondered if I was sick again and I wondered if I was going crazy, not really able to explain my sudden sadness.

Relieved to be invited to a party to celebrate the new year, I pulled myself together, slipped into my brand new hand-sewn pantsuit, and headed out to celebrate New Year's Eve. I was unaccompanied by André since he had to work and wouldn't have felt so comfortable in this group of teachers and government workers anyway. I knew very few of the guests, each of them formally dressed, men in suits, hopelessly wrinkled, and women in Western professional attire. It seemed more like a convention gathering than a New Year's party—a contrast to the colorful and beautiful outfits at Christmas. I was the only non-Togolese present and felt clumsy and self-conscious. The scene was so incongruous, suits in such hot weather. I wondered if the status as *fonctionnaire*, a civil service employee, demanded a level of formality. It felt so artificial. I tried to control my squirminess.

We sat in a silent circle, getting up to help ourselves to servings of spaghetti from a big pot and a can of Coke or Fanta, fancy, expensive drinks reserved for festive occasions. Mercifully, music began and we all rose as men began asking women to dance. After each song, we changed partners. It felt like a really awkward prom in seventh grade, such a contrast to the joy and spontaneity of the dancing outside on Christmas. Our engineer-host had fallen asleep in his chair beside a pregnant lady. It was hard to stay awake until midnight. Still, no one introduced himself or asked my name. Instead, at song's end, each of my partners clapped, bowed and thanked me for the dance. "*Bien dansé, trés bien dansé!*"

At midnight, our host came to life. He got our attention and declared with levity, "*Nous sommes dans l'année 1972.*" The New Year had begun! People responded in polite applause then we bowed our heads in silent prayer. Out of nowhere a group of uniformed soldiers marched into the center of the room, raising their trumpets and bleating out a few marches. The tunes were flat, the instruments squeaky, but everyone smiled. As the trumpeters departed, the group assumed two circles, one facing in, the other facing out. Our circles rotated in opposite directions exchanging greetings. I followed along, mystified by the unspoken script that they knew and I didn't.

"*Bonsoir, Monsieur le Professeur. Comment allez-vous?*"

"*Salut, Monsieur le Directeur! Bonne fete!*"

"*Halo, Mees Pike. J'espère que tout va bien.*" A colleague from the public high school wished me well. The music resumed, and gradually, the easy rocks and rolls of soukous music from *Zaire* and highlife music from Ghana softened the mood and we relaxed. Before long we were moving more easily and speaking to each other more spontaneously.

"*Bonne année!*" we wished each other "Happy new year!" as the crowd dwindled and we all prepared to head home.

I heard "*Bonne année!*" throughout the next day as men gathered in clusters outside our compound, drinking *Bière Bénin* and shouting repeatedly to passers-by. The odd weather and strange customs kept me feeling fragile and far away as a new trimester at school began. A heavy spirit stayed with me for the first few weeks of the new year. In letters home, I complained about missing my friends and family, about how hard it was to be so far away. "Only one-and-a-half years until I can come home!" I begged my mom to visit and I set out an early plan to meet a friend during the upcoming summer break.

Fortunately, the demands of teaching overrode the blues. With a steady routine at Adèle, I was curious to investigate just how different teaching was at a public school. I proposed a one-time exchange with a teacher at the *lycée*, a fellow who'd been one of my more cheerful New Year's Eve dance partners. He agreed to the idea, I got a "*D'accord*" from the nuns and arrived for a guest lesson at the local crowded high school. Wading through open corridors and smiling at curious students, I made my way to the classroom and spent the first few minutes cleaning an illegible blackboard with a dusty rag, searching for chalk and greeting the fifty or so classmates, three to a bench. I proceeded to teach by repeating some of my most successful lessons, orchestrating a variety of oral drills, introducing a Jazz Chant and topping off the lesson with "I'm a Little Teapot." Students chitchatted to each other the entire hour, likely concluding that my lesson couldn't possibly have been serious. I sang, I smiled too much, I had them talk aloud, all strange activities in a traditional classroom. I concluded that I was fortunate to be teaching at

Collège Adèle. Legible chalkboards, ventilated classrooms and attentive students were not necessarily the norm. Increasingly appreciative of how dedicated and efficient my nun-colleagues were, I took note of the small classes and high standards and even the improvement in my French. My students were excited to have me back after their brief experience with a local teacher. I felt gratified and settled in.

Perhaps partly inspired by our trip to Lomé, Sina decided to spend more time studying. I could sometimes count on Afia, the only girl in my landlord Claude's brood, who continued to offer her housekeeping services when she'd finished her chores for the family. But she was rarely finished with her household duties. I had a conversation with Oncle about sending her to school.

"*Ça ne vaut pas la peine.*" It wasn't worthwhile to send girls to school, he explained. I held my breath, hoping I could convince him otherwise as my credibility as teacher, neighbor, woman increased. Maybe next year I could take Afia to Lomé with me, I secretly plotted. With Sina studying and Afia rarely available, I hired a new boy, Florent. He was smart and eager and at the top of his English class, so we communicated easily. A new year!

It was truly West African winter. The last of the millet stalks in our yard were cut and burned and we were visible to passers-by from three different directions. I was adjusting, once again, to an even greater lack of privacy. Hard to believe, but I was getting used to it. The harmattan wind blew all day long, a dry, cold wind in the morning and night. It dried my skin, chapped my lips and continued to fill my world with fine sooty dust. During this time of year the sky was so blue and the sun was so bright I couldn't go outside without sunglasses. I adjusted to the weather extremes, showering during the daytime, gently shaking sand out of my typewriter and blowing silt from my stationery before I stamped it with my new seal.

Oh no! Now what?! Was it possible I had poison oak? I woke up one morning with an itchy rash all over my face, my eyes swollen shut. Ice

Sina in his new African outfit

bags helped, but I needed another few hours before going outside. I was afraid I'd scare all the children with such a swollen face. Had the weather brought this on? Though everyone talked about the dramatic weather conditions, it didn't affect anyone else's daily routine. Work for them proceeded normally. Hoping for a quick recovery, I stepped outside to glimpse that beautiful blue sky. Sometimes, in ever more frequent flashes, it seemed as if I'd been here all my life.

What does the bus station in Accra most resemble? The caravan of a huge circus that has come to a brief stop. It is colorful, and there is music...A bus in Accra has a wooden body, its roof resting on four posts. Because there are open walls, a pleasant breeze cools the ride. In this climate, the value of a breeze is never to be taken for granted.

—RYSZARD KAPUSCINSKI, *The Shadow of the Sun: My African Life*

BRANCHING OUT

IN THE BEGINNING, my girlfriends in Togo seemed random and far-flung. I remarked frequently that they were nothing like my friends at home, though all were American and most were Peace Corps volunteers whom I'd met in Lomé or run into passing through town. You'd think we'd have shared lots of similarities, but all I saw were differences. No one I met in Togo resembled Evelyn, hip, beautiful and adventuresome, also a Californian, and my best friend from training. Girlfriends here

On vacation in Ghana

were so uncool, so eager to follow rules and wear such unimaginative clothes, a sure sign of their lack of liberal politics. Why did they wear what everyone else wore—the kind of clothes you'd buy in the store? It seemed so unoriginal. In spite of my reluctance to name them pals or join their circles, girlfriends were surprisingly generous with me. Sarah, a health volunteer, promised to reserve her house for me at the end of her two-year stint.

"Oh, Sarah! Thank you so much!" I gushed. The ease and convenience of my centrally located home was wearing off. I wearied of the constant noise, the relentless gawking. I jumped at the chance to move into her place in a few months' time and promised my current neighbors, practically family now, that I'd visit often. Sarah promised to leave me her cassette tape collection too, gifting me comfortable space, privacy and the music of Afrobeat's founder, Fela Kuti. I was beginning to love his endless songs and angry rhythmic bellowing against injustice and government corruption.

Most of the Peace Corps volunteers I got to meet were in health or education. Because of the different work, we didn't get to know each other unless we lived in the same towns. Another health volunteer I met early on, Sally, was chatty and fun. I was hopeful we'd do lots of things together. But our schedules didn't jive at all and I discovered that her preoccupations were a world away from mine. She was consumed with rural health challenges while I was preoccupied with classroom management and how to teach irregular verbs. She was learning Kabré in order to explain neonatal health and family planning. I was learning Kabré to buy groceries. The biggest difference between us, however, and the one that caught my breath, was her mastery at living nimbly and working so effectively in distant villages, creating her own schedule, scouting out new groups of women who were willing to commit to a brief class, and then locating a shady gathering place within walking distance to meet. All of these complicated tasks were done for me. I was served students, a strict schedule and even a room with desks, chairs and chalkboard to teach them. I couldn't imagine having to recruit audiences, determine a timeframe and negotiate venues all on my own. So, regrettably, Sally and I didn't get together often.

Rosalyn, another promising friend and Peace Corps volunteer in education, was married and pregnant. She and her volunteer husband invited me for dinner now and then and we talked about common acquaintances in town, successful English lessons and recipes. Her religious tendencies put me off as she directed grace before our meal and often said "Lord be praised!' and "Hallelujah!" Rosalyn was from New Orleans so I saw these expressions as cultural rather than religious and I tried hard to befriend her, especially because she was the only other American woman living nearby. But she was glued to her handsome acquiescent husband and they didn't venture far from their spacious concrete home. Their focus was on each other and the coming baby, not on the people, places and peculiarities of their new culture. My other nearby American girlfriend, Nancy, had just joined her French boyfriend in Lama-Kara. Nancy wanted to be useful, so she landed a part-time teaching job and came to me for advice. I told her what I knew, helped her design a lesson, rattled off choral response techniques and shared a few tricks to manage large classes.

"I can't tell you how helpful this is!" she exclaimed. Nancy and I hit it off from the start, but she was too busy in her compound of French friends and couldn't spend much time with me. And I was intimidated by the French volunteers in Lama-Kara. I didn't understand their jokes and when they weren't joking, I couldn't keep up with their French.

Our vacation route

Something about Polly, my square roommate in Lomé, pulled me to her as time went on. She was disciplined, talented and as serious as I was about doing a good job of teaching. Although we lived in different towns, our school schedules matched and she was curious about Togo, its neighbors and the African continent. We may not have agreed politically, but I was beginning to appreciate her. What's more, like me, she needed a friend. We decided to take our first real vacation together, after my Christmas trip to Lomé left me wanting to branch out. We were anxious to flee Togo and escape the pressure of always speaking French and being so visible in our communities. We wanted to take a break from the relentless demands of first-year teaching, so decided to travel the length of neighboring Ghana, the Anglophone (English-speaking) country stretched up against the west side of Togo. Like Togo, Ghana is taller than it is wide. We wanted to cruise its length heading north, just like a Ghanaian would travel. We gathered a few travel tips from local friends, some well-worn maps, exchanged West African francs for Ghanaian *cedis* and made a plan to take taxis, busses and open-sided vans called mammy wagons. We'd work our way north to towns, scouting out modest hostels along the way. We imagined that the adventure would be easy and straightforward since Ghana's national language was English. We'd keep our eyes open for crafts, cloth and beads. I was eager to visit a tie-dye center I'd learned about.

Our scheme was to proceed in segments, along a string of major towns until we reached Bawku, the sleepy way station for people on trucks, vans, busses or camels heading to Upper Volta, Mali and beyond into the Sahara. We hoped to continue north to Upper Volta, perhaps, make a sharp turn and cross the border, back into Togo, turning south or east to head home. It was a brilliant plan, we thought, and one which would give us bragging rights to having traveled the length of two countries. We'd return to our homes and teaching, knowledgeable about local travel while having spent time in a part of English-speaking Africa. We counseled each other as we prepared.

"No drinking the water!"

"Stay flexible! We have plenty of time—school doesn't begin for two weeks!"

"And don't forget the importance of resilience!" Words from the Peace Corps invitation letter reverberated. "A Peace Corps teaching assignment requires ingenuity, flexibility and patience." The advice applied to traveling, not just teaching. Actually, I realized, it applied to everything here.

We deduced that there wasn't much we couldn't endure. We'd lived in Togo just shy of six months and felt like experts.

"Ghana can't be so different from Togo, can it?" It was bound to be easier.

"What a great break this will be!" Polly cheered.

"What a fun adventure!" I concurred. As if beginning a relay loop, I departed Lama-Kara, traveled south to pick up Polly and together we proceeded to Lomé. We went west from Lomé across the border to Ghana, as I'd previously done with Sina, and then headed into the unknown, happy and optimistic. We made our first stop in Accra, the noisy, crowded capital city, eager to track down some good restaurants. The traffic was surprisingly unsettling and confusing.

"I guess development isn't always so great," Polly remarked, reacting to Ghana's reputation at being more modern than Togo.

"I miss the slow pace and friendly people of Togo," I complained. "And we haven't even been here two days!"

"Accra's so rush-rush and intense." I was continuing to warm up to Polly, appreciative of her willingness to entertain this adventure, noting that we were beginning to agree more. She wasn't so rigid after all, it seemed to me. We bought chocolate and ogled at the abundance of enticing restaurants. I began to respect the city's energy but was struck by the pervasive stench of open gutters. Lomé was graced by a similar sewage system, but dirt roads and fewer people made Togo's capital much less stinky. We ventured beyond the city center to visit the university, leering at signs and books in English. I gathered postcards of an expansive and well laid out campus and observed students of many backgrounds talk in lively clusters, sit on grassy patches or walk purposely about carrying books. The university must be one advantage of development; Togo's university was yet to develop.

On Day 2, we were ready to begin our journey upcountry and made our way to a noisy car park on the outskirts of Accra where we found a small line of vehicles heading north. Travel in Africa proceeded gradually, in general, one link at a time. Vehicles didn't depart until they were full of passengers, and then there were any number of delays *en route*: a flat tire to repair, a sick passenger to assist, a tired driver who stopped by the side of the road and helped himself to a short nap. There were route hazards too, such as sudden holes and missing roadways, moving crowds of villagers, herds of cattle, goats, sheep, and oncoming recklessly driven vehicles. We were aware of these possibilities, cheerful even, and climbed onto a mammy wagon that was half-full, promising an imminent departure. I was sure this would be easier than my Christmastime train ride to Lomé.

"TOOT-TOOT-TOOT!"

Vehicles in West Africa had distinct personalities, empty or full. Their lyrical horns and carnival colors were a steady source of amusement. They careened around road bends and sped up and down the length of countries along the Gold Coast with decorated names of popular singers or religious heroes, moralistic proverbs or Bible quotes. Our bus, *Pélé*, sporting colors of the Brazilian flag and plentiful dents, was typical. We hopped aboard and sat at the end of a wooden bench where we could clutch the heavy metal poles that framed the vehicle. The jolting from sharp turns, dips and bumps of the dirt roads necessitated holding on to something. The adjacent pole as a handle was more stationery than the arms or shoulders of passengers crowding in around us. There were no sides on most of the mini-buses like ours, exposing us to the inevitable heat, breeze and dust as travelling proceeded. This was nearly everyone's way of getting from one place to another outside major cities. We tied our hair back in ponytails and smiled as our fellow passengers filled the benches, pushing their way in with chickens, bins of potatoes, fruit and babies.

Our first stop was Kumasi. We found a comfortable hostel and enjoyed a dinner of chewy brochettes at a local "chicken bar." After a good night's sleep we caught a taxi to the bus stop for our second leg of the trip. We were on the mammy wagon at 8, all set for a 9AM departure.

"This is great!" Polly exclaimed. Yep. Fun trip so far. We continued to sit and wait, and though the hours passed, I figured we'd be off before too long. But the wait continued. More passengers embarked with more cargo and the wagon was full to overflowing. We were hot pressing up against each other and anxious to get going, but Polly and I were the only ones with a sense of urgency. No one else seemed to mind the wait.

"The driver will join us momentarily," someone told us eventually, "as soon as he finishes his prayers." We finally departed at 3PM, after a seven-hour wait. The delayed departure had us traveling through the night. The weather cooled down, but because of the dark we didn't get to see the countryside and we didn't sleep.

"I haven't slept a wink," Polly told me somewhere around 3AM. "You?" I hadn't slept either. The road had become a "washboard", ridged deeply from too much traffic. Our driver tried to attain a speed that "flew" over the tops of the ridges, but was forced to slow down when he spotted deep holes or oncoming cars. We felt each jolt. I understood finally why our French friends in Togo and the nuns were so fond of talking about kidneys. "*Mes reins!!*" they'd complained when feeling indisposed. They must have been traveling on mammy-wagons.

"My lower back aches," I whispered to Polly. "I think I finally know where my kidneys are." At 4AM we began clutching our mid-sections, bending forward and bracing our bodies for the next section of rough road. The bumps became excruciating. How did the bus survive? How did our fellow passengers do this regularly? They seemed to take it all in stride; we were both painfully uncomfortable.

"Oh-h-h," I moaned through a whisper to Polly.

"This is awful," she agreed. Everyone around us was sleeping, their heads bobbing on their chests or against others' shoulders. At 5AM we reached Bolgatanga, three-fourths of the way to the top of the country and our destination for this leg of the journey. We stood, finally, shook our bodies alert as the sun rose and stepped off the bus.

"Madam! Madam!" Someone called.

"Oh my gosh!" Polly exclaimed. "A vendor at this early hour?!" Sure enough, a short friendly man with bracelets strung along both forearms approached. He'd made a beeline for us, the only white passengers, as we clutched our bags and hobbled forward. He followed us to a nearby tree and thrust his arms our way, displaying circular half-inch strips of smooth brown leather edged with white stitching. We had no energy to chase the guy away and the bracelets were so simple, natural and inexpensive that each of us bought two. In spite of no sleep, our spirits were cheered up by our purchases, a beautiful sky and the cool air of early morning. Sunrise greeted us with billowing white clouds against a lavender backdrop. We sat under the tree and tried to rest at the car park contemplating our next move.

"Let's keep going!" we agreed after deciding that Bolgatanga seemed to have little to offer. We drank coffee to shed the lack-of-sleep haze. But by the time we boarded the bus for the last leg upcountry, we weren't talking much and our bodies ached. I hoped we could catch a quick nap before Bawku. I was feeling sick to my stomach and Polly was looking pale and grim. We got going, but the final stretch north was full of more bumps and sharp turns, so no naps. We were too groggy to be fearful of the fast driving.

"I'm not sure I want to stop in Bawku either," I ventured to Polly after bumping my head on the bar behind our seat for the third time. "I miss Togo. It's so dry and flat and dusty here. There can't be any interesting places to visit." Suddenly Togo felt like home and Togolese French seemed more comforting than Ghanaian English.

"Yeah," Polly concurred. I wondered privately why we'd come all this way to feel miserable and see nothing. "But let's wait til we get to Bawku— maybe we'll be happily surprised." Polly was so optimistic. I looked forward to approaching the border region where Ghana met Upper Volta to the north and Togo to the east and wondered if the scenery would change. But as we headed into drier countryside, the road became more torturous. By the time we got to Bawku and disembarked, finally, I felt weak and nauseous. The sun was blasting its dry heat on a dusty, deserted, desolate car park. I took my first look at Polly in daylight and gasped.

"Awww! Do I look like you? That bad?! Your hair, your clothes, <u>everything</u> is covered in dust!" We looked like raccoons, eyes framed by dirt. We both mustered a laugh and propped sunglasses atop our dusty heads to take a photo, then settled on a rock in the partial shade. A few people walked by and I spotted a kid with a huge jug of water on his head, but no other activity. It was very hot.

"I want to go home. I miss André," I wailed softly. "This is no fun." We noticed a Land Rover and were told by the driver that it was heading to Dapango, in Togo, in two hours.

Covered in dust from our mammy wagon adventure

"Perfect!" we chorused and sat back down on our rock. This had been a west African public transport marathon. My back and body ached and we were covered in dust. But we didn't regret it, playfully acknowledging that we hadn't seen much more than the inside of bumpy vehicles. It was part of the adventure! Two hours later there was no sign of the driver and we lost enthusiasm. With nothing else to do, we waited. I was feeling worse, ill, and discouraged about the trip. Someone said something about the Ghana-Togo border being closed. Oh no! We felt abandoned, in barren country. We watched random vendors walk around selling sweet warm Coca Cola. Remember, the water is unsafe. We bought a third bottle of Coke. A couple of people approached us but Polly couldn't understand them and I was feeling too sick to pay attention. I was dizzy, weak and hungry. Around noon a friendly man in a sleeveless tunic approached.

"GreetINGS ladIES!" he accented the final syllables of each word, smiling broadly and bending forward solicitously. He had a suspicious I-want-something-from-you manner about him.

"Good day!" Polly did all the talking. "We're going to Dapango." She tried to dismiss him by seeming purposeful.

"Oh, can I help you?"

"No thanks."

"Well, I'd like to offer to help your friend. She doesn't look well. She needs to come home with me. Here, here's some money." He pulled 30 cedis, roughly $35, out of his pocket. I was jolted alert by this gesture. When Polly refused his offer, he pulled out more bills.

"What do you intend to do if I go home with you?" I asked, hunched over and suspicious of his offer. "No thanks, Mister. I have my friend here to help me." I didn't understand why he wanted to pay to take me home. We didn't have enough shared language to explain ourselves, so the Mister finally walked away, but the encounter stirred questions. Did he truly want to help? Did his offer of money make him more trustworthy to a westerner? Was he trustworthy?

We were into afternoon now. No driver, no foreseeable way out of this inhospitable empty car park. I didn't like Ghana. I wanted to go home. At about 3PM I spotted something that took me by surprise. A white woman drove up and was getting out of a nearby car. I wondered if she could help us. Desperate now, I stood up and hobbled over to her.

"Hello, ma'am? Excuse my appearance, but I need some advice." I explained our dilemma and asked if she knew of any transport going to Togo. She was a small woman, simply dressed. She said she lived in town and after a pause told me to gather our bags and come with her.

"Wow! Really?!" Polly and I were relieved and bundled into her car in the scorching afternoon heat. We drove away from the car park, nearly tearful with gratitude for the warm breeze on our grimy faces. Not for a second had we mistrusted this woman. For one, she was American and spoke English. She was also sympathetic. Compatriot strangers had a way of becoming fast friends far from home. During the brief ride, we learned that Addie was an American missionary working and had been living in Bawku for many years. We parked outside a thick, clay-walled compound, climbed out of the car into a cool foyer and met Addie's partner, Pauli, who grabbed our bags and ushered us to two bedrooms. We laughed about the similarities in names, Pauli and Polly.

"Meredith's not feeling well." Polly generously directed their attention to my near faint condition. I thought she must be feeling equally bad and appreciated her getting me cared for first. I took my first shower in four days, was treated to a small meal and sank into the softest, most comfortable bed I could remember. I drifted into a deep slumber while Polly and our two new friends got to know each other. I couldn't believe our great good luck at coming upon these two women.

At 2AM I was awakened by what sounded like hundreds of drummers pounding out rhythms right under my window. What was it? Where was I? Alarmed and disoriented, I sat up in bed. Addie and Pauli's housekeeper knocked on my door and peeked in to tell me that everyone in the missionary compound was celebrating Easter Sunday. Oh yes! Easter! After a brief sleep, we all got up, watched the sun rise and listened to jubilant choruses of drumming and singing. I felt better after a few hours' rest and Polly, Addie and Pauli were friends now, having shared all sorts of information about living and teaching in Togo, the life of missionaries, and Ghana's promising future. This chance encounter was a new beginning to our adventure, I thought, echoing the hope of the Easter theme. Our new friends invited us to join them on some Easter morning visits.

"We've seen so little on this trip," we told them. "It would be great to get a sense of how people live." The four of us hopped in the car and drove about a half hour over flat dusty fields spotting clumps of trees in the distance. I couldn't imagine living here in such an arid region. We arrived at a clay-walled cluster of round grass-topped structures. Women in long skirts and children in school uniforms rushed out to meet us when they heard the car. It may have been Easter morning, but everyday activities were in progress at this village. Addie had business to do with two of the families so Pauli walked us around, introducing us to residents. We met a 10-year old boy ironing. He kept the iron hot by regularly filling it with chunks of burning coal. We walked past a mother pig feeding her six piglets in the hot sun. Off in a corner of the compound we watched an elderly man, seated on the ground against a skinny tree trunk, weaving a thick grass mat by folding long stiff wands of straw back and forth. We learned that he was blind. We took a few souvenir photos, returned home and prepared for Easter lunch and our departure. We hoped to get across the border to Togo before dark. Addie and Pauli drove us back to the car park and we found a ride to Dapango right away.

"Thank you so much!" Polly and I were effusive in a round of good-byes. "Our visit to Bawku and meeting you have been the high point of the trip!" We felt refreshed and ready to return home. Our brief visit had expanded our appreciation for Ghana.

We entered Togo and got to Dapango in the afternoon and learned that there was a ride to Lama-Kara at 6PM. Transportation was finally beginning to go smoothly. Although the truck was delayed until 7:30, the first leg proceeded easily enough and we unloaded passengers in Kandé, the town directly north of Lama-Kara. Back to Togo and back to French! It was good to be returning home. We climbed back into the driver's cabin, enabled by our privilege of being white, promised to pay for our enhanced comfort, and anxiously anticipated our arrival home. But when I looked over at the driver, I was shocked.

"Polly! Look! The driver's asleep!"

"Oh no! So close to home! Just one more leg!" We attempted to wake him, slamming the door a few times, singing, talking loudly, but it took 15 minutes for the driver to revive. He shook his head, rubbed his eyes, and pulled out onto the main road. Finally! Almost home. We exchanged smiles. But instead of speeding up, he slowed down, pulled over, parked, got out of the truck. He walked into the nearest compound to continue sleeping. Arrrgh! It was 11PM and we were only 45 minutes from our destination! Once again, none of the other passengers seemed the least bit troubled. Completely exasperated with all the unpredictable delays, impatient to be home, tired of long waits, we climbed out of the truck cabin and decided that we'd do better finding another way home. We'd hitchhike.

"He might sleep all night. We've got to get home!" We announced to our fellow passengers. About twenty minutes later, a huge top-heavy truck approached, barreling south down the dirt road. We flagged it down and in a mixture of French, Kabré and sign language, we indicated that we needed a lift to the next town, Lama-Kara. The cabin was full. There must have been 12 people in the cabin crowded next to the driver. No Yovo privileges here.

"We'll stand in the back!" we offered, practically screaming and looking hopefully at the twenty or so passengers in the cargo section standing and holding on to each other. Everyone in the cabin had an opinion about our proposal, but in the end, after a long exchange of comments we couldn't understand, we dragged ourselves and our small bags onto the back of the truck where we sidled up to a truckload of strangers. With nothing to sit on or brace ourselves against, we clutched each other's clothing, arms, shoulders and hands as the huge truck lumbered back onto the dirt road and proceeded south in the middle of the night. I figured we could manage this for less than an hour. But shortly after our departure, we felt wet heavy drops on our heads and peered skyward. It was raining!

"Take this!" Polly handed me a towel and we huddled under it, completely unprepared for the cold and wet of riding in the back of a cargo truck near midnight in the rain. By the time we got to Lama-Kara, a long hour later, we were sopping wet, exhausted, hungry, weak and demoralized. No more adventures! No more African travel!

"Polly, I can't find my house key." I mumbled, scrounging in pockets and my bag. Why was returning home so difficult?! Weary and frustrated, we decided to to go to André's, necessarily waking him to ask for my second key.

"Clap! Clap-clap-clap! André?!" We called softly over the scratches of crickets, trying not to awaken his neighbors. He finally answered our tentative knocking and appeared at the door half asleep. We entered, wrapped in wet towels with dripping hair, exchanged a quick greeting, brief explanation and almost immediately crashed on the floor of his small living room. We were relieved to be home, or almost home, and we fell asleep right away.

The next morning we sat outside in the sunshine and told André and his compound neighbors about our adventure.

"It was a disaster!" Polly exclaimed, smiling at the same time. "We've had enough of African travel!" I agreed with her about the travel but was aware that the challenging vacation had shown me a new side of Polly. She'd been open and willing to try this silly plot. She'd never become annoyed at the interminable delays. She'd been cheerful and resilient the whole time. She'd been caring and considerate toward me the entire trip. I looked down at my two leather bracelets, twirled them on my wrist and concluded that my travel companion was no longer a default pal. Polly was a real friend.

Fanta, the girl who carried water for us and washed our clothes, was next to arrive... I was surprised to see her, so shy with us, sprawl across our bench, prop her head on her elbow, and start up a flirtation with Zeeay, one of our neighbor's sons. As more adults arrived Fanta was chased off the bench so the men could sit down. Nonchalantly, she moved into one of our few chairs, which we were saving for important elders, and continued her conversation with Zeeay without a pause. He looked positively charmed.

—**CAROL SPINDEL**, *In the Shadow of the Sacred Grove*

HELP

DAILY ROUTINES HUMMED to a predictable and comfortable rhythm nine months in. I loved my life in Togo. I often caught myself thinking *je m'y habitue,* I'm used to this. The making-do with improvised tools and the willing acceptance of few once-familiar conveniences turned each day into a problem-solving puzzle. How to bake without an oven? Keep bats out of my house at night? Be prepared for tomorrow's classes before an early sunset or finish lesson plans bent over the dim light of my kerosene lantern? Happy and optimistic, I embraced most trials: the bugs, the persistent gawkers, the unyielding vendors. One night Sundia got too close to the fire and singed her whiskers. Another time Claude spotted a snake in my garden. Sometimes there was a mouse scurrying back and forth in the kitchen. I was only momentarily alarmed. As for the demanding and time-consuming tasks of daily life even with lots of support, I imagined that I was on a long camping trip. I loved camping.

But I surely couldn't do everything by or for myself. Living like a local, and comfortably, required help: cooks, cleaners, carpenters and *boys.* Boys were a practical solution to the sweeping, dusting, and washing each day required. They cleaned our motorized bicycles, mobylettes, removed ominous insects from high places, bought the onion I forgot, regularly replenished kerosene lanterns, gave unsolicited tips on preparing tomato sauce, kept the mosquito count down while correctly pronouncing "*Pardon?*" in the local language. Boys were *Les Grandes Guides*, living, breathing translators of culture who were more accessible and accurate than any helpful booklet. In a country of vast regional differences, *boys* could advise and interpret frequent mysteries.

Extremely uncomfortable with the idea of hired help, I was caught between guarding my time alone and yearning to fit in, with a keen desire to be mistaken for a local. I yearned to be an insider, not an outsider. I embraced the Peace Corps' goal of "community integration" by trying to live and behave as a native resident would. So under pressure from my Peace Corps predecessors and compound mates, I developed an informal arrangement with the first two boys who approached me for work. Sina, my compound "brother" and a high school student, was my first *boy*. When his studies became demanding, I encouraged him to spend more time reviewing lessons and I accepted the help of another local student. *Florent* swept and dusted every day. I was proud of my willingness to fit in, and went so far as to send my laundry to a professional, a *blanchisseur*. I figured I could afford these luxuries. They totalled $4.50 a month.

Florent was punctual, efficient and spoke enough English to have interesting conversations, but I really wanted to hire Afia, the compound's only girl. She seemed to have a bit of free time and I wanted to show her brothers, cousins and uncle that girls and women were worth the investment of teaching and training. After all, I taught at a girls' school, so it seemed the society was beginning to acknowledge the contributions educated women could make. I'd accepted Afia's help informally, during her intermittent visits when I'd been washing dishes, cooking or writing letters, but I hoped to take her in for more regular duties. In some cases, *boys* could be girls. So when Florent could no longer help me, I hired Afia.

Afia hadn't ever gone to school and she didn't speak French or English, so I tried to show her how she could expand her skills beyond dishwash-

Afia

ing support. I relied mostly on sign language, acting out the motions of tasks I wanted her to learn. Watching how others directed their *boys* had scared me. They shouted, insulted, berated. Not me.

"Afia, do you, uh, think you could sweep under my bed?" I asked tentatively, bending down and moving the long straw broom in a sweeping motion. She stood facing me, eyes wide, completely expressionless. Did she understand? Did she hate sweeping under beds? Perhaps there was bad luck associated with dust. I'd been cautioned about throwing my hair out the window.

"Sorcerers can gather your hair, your nails even, and use them against you if someone wishes you evil," Togolese friends had told me. Maybe dust had witchcraft power too.

I handed the broom to Afia, and she indicated that she understood, proceeding to sweep in excruciatingly slow motion. I let her be. After nearly a half hour of sluggish sweeping I had to figure out something else for her to do. I left dishes for her to wash because the books to rearrange and the front steps to clear of dust and sand were beyond my nonverbal teaching ability. At the end of a few weeks, Afia was able to go about a few limited chores relatively independently and she began to teach me some skills. Thanks to her help, I improved the balancing act of taking showers in an open-air stall. I poured large hollowed gourds of water, calabashes, over my head, soaped down, rinsed off with the calabash, and grabbed the towel without dropping anything, soap, gourd or towel. I also became skillful at not being seen by neighbors as I dashed from the shower to my house. Afia was so nimble with gourd-dipping and towel-balancing that I tried to mimic her ease. She was also amazingly strong for her short stature. She carried boxes, basins, bags effortlessly, lifting them swiftly atop her head and walking sometimes many kilometers. Now that the rain had stopped, she helped me set a rhythm of boiling and filtering river water so that it didn't run out. She insisted through finger-pointing and knotted eyebrows that I keep an adequate supply in my huge ceramic filter on the kitchen counter. All of this I learned by watching her and exchanging nods and glances of agreement. When I wanted her to repeat an action, I moved my arm in a circle. "Do it again, Afia. Show me once more!" She usually understood my nonverbal requests.

Afia's tutelage gave me courage to try out a few new experiments on my own. I made my own yogurt, letting the diluted powdered milk ferment atop my *frigo*, the miniature refrigerator. It took a day to achieve the right texture. *Voila!* Homemade yogurt and short, sweet bananas were my daily breakfast. I produced pulpy orange batches of mango *compôte* and even figured out how to bake cakes in a sand oven. My repertoire was limited to banana and applesauce. And banana cake was only possible once or twice a month when I could buy fresh eggs. I poured batter into a cake pan then lowered it into a large stockpot lined with sand. Bracing it on an upturned empty tomato sauce container, I turned on the burner and waited for an hour or so. If the stove didn't run out of *gaz* or if I didn't run out of patience, I lifted the cover of the pot to discover a tasty cake. Sometimes, though, I ended up with a mound of gummy dough. I ran a one-to-one win rate with my cakes, one success for every failure. Not bad given I didn't have an oven. And when successful, I always shared small pieces of sweet cake with my neighbors.

Most of my compound mates were Oncle Claude's immediate or extended family members. In addition, there was a young mother who herded her gang of four children from one end of the dusty compound to the other. Two of them were babies, twins, whom she kept tied on her body all the time, one nursing on her front and the other sleeping on her back. I suppose she had a husband, but she never spoke of him and I never saw him. All I knew was that she worked hard with those kids, cleaning and cooking and nursing and carrying. While I spent most of my time inside, all the others spent most of their time outside. Compound activity ebbed and flowed with neighbors, children, family members and friends showing up unexpectedly, townspeople dropping by and occasionally my friends passing through. I stopped trying to understand exactly who was related to whom and when they might be visiting. I just enjoyed everyone's abounding cheerfulness, curiosity and good food.

"*Venez Mees! Il faut manger!*" One of the children called me to come eat. Most evenings I had dinner with my neighbors, usually 8-10 of us sitting around a bowl of fish, meat or chicken stew. We dipped small fingers full of patte, pounded yam or millet from another large bowl, into the sauce and smiled as we plopped tasty nuggets into our mouths. The spicier, the better. Men usually ate separately and they were usually sweating by the end of the meal. Most believed that spicy foods kept us healthy and cooled us down, providing relief from the relentless heat. Mama Twins approached as we finished one night and announced something in a language I didn't understand. One of the kids translated, telling me she'd be making treats for us the next day. Everyone cheered, encouraging her to make enough for us to have two or three or four.

The following day's treat was *kuli kuli*, peanut candy. Madame ground peanuts, added some flour and sugar, and mixed it all together until the dough was soft and pliable. Then she pressed the khaki colored mound flat on the surface of a large smooth stone, cutting small squares. With flat hands she rolled each square into a long cylinder then dropped it into boiling oil. I joined the crowd of young spectators as she assembled the sizzling batch of candy. Yum! We gobbled our pieces down before a new plate appeared.

"*Doucement, doucement!*" Mama Twins told us to slow down. The kids jumped and danced and ran back and forth across the compound. I was always included in these spontaneous celebrations, regularly invited to partake of gifts of oranges, usually yellow, bananas, always miniature, or dried fish, typically smelly. My neighbors were bountiful.

Afia, my part-time girl-boy, was among the throng, observing more than participating, eyes cast away. I noticed how skinny she was, all arms and legs, with her hair in small, tight spirals close to her head. She looked twelve but was fifteen. She whispered when she spoke to her uncle, my landlord and immediate neighbor. She and I continued communicating with my one expression in Kabré (*Alafia-we?* How are you?), and a modified version of charades. I noticed increasingly that something about Afia made her seem shifty. Was it only with me that she seemed evasive? She couldn't stand still, darted about from one spot to the other, easily distracted by all the activity. When we talked with others around us, her eyes avoided mine. She was shy, I explained to myself, restless. She'd been so discouraged by everyone else. I'd teach her some skills and hoped her confidence would increase. I was sure that both of us would be more comfortable once I was able to use language to communicate with her.

But inside my small house bent over her straw broom she worked too inconsistently, sometimes slow then sometimes too fast, spewing dust over cushions and countertops, until I stopped her, once again demonstrating how to take long, smooth strokes. It was like this with everything: I had to stop and re-teach her how to wash and rinse dishes, how to empty the small basket of garbage, how not to move my books, try on my bracelets or rifle through my closet. I smiled and believed that if she trusted me, some day she'd become my fulltime boy and eventually be as helpful as both Sina and Florent had been.

Afia was deeply curious about me and my things, hanging about long after her tasks were completed, gazing longingly at my collection of earrings, my beads, pens and pencils, my sewing kit. She always asked for something and this made me uncomfortable. She was a girl, after all. Her male cousins hadn't been interested in the same kinds of things. At the beginning I was too embarrassed to turn down her bold requests. I've got more chocolate and plenty of pens and pencils, I'd say to myself. I could give her something. But after a steady stream of gifts upon request, I held back.

"Sorry, Afia, not today," I learned to say and simultaneously gesture, resisting the urge to justify my refusal. "Sorry, Afia, these earrings are special. Sorry, Afia, this pen is important for my work." Although I smiled, she understood my refusal and smiled in return. We finally eased into a routine, my informal girl-boy and I. She steadied her sweeping and stopped asking for things. This enabled me to begin offering her kindness which I was pleased to do, especially since she was treated so terribly by everyone else. I overheard her uncle or her older cousin or another adult in the compound continually pelt orders at her:

"A RAG, Afia! NOW! Bring me a rag!"

"Matches, Afia! Where are the matches?! HURRY!"

"You stupid girl! Why don't you wash this more carefully?"

"Choose an onion that isn't rotten!"

"Don't take so long!! You're like a tortoise." I believed that if I was more respectful to her, she would respond with greater pride in her work and more self-confidence in her manner. I was determined help her.

With all my household help, both compensated and voluntary, I had more time to devote to lesson-planning and corrections. I didn't even have to wash my clothes. While Afia helped me in the house, an elderly gentleman walked to my place from across the river every week to pick up my shirts and dresses. He returned them washed and ironed and neatly stacked. As if to advertise his impeccable service, he appeared in a sleek white boubou each time. I felt a bit like a princess with my staff of helpers, convinced that I was offering employment opportunities to various villagers in spite of the initial discomfort with having people work for me.

One day I noticed that more than half of my underpants were missing. That was odd. Had I put them in the wrong place? Did I leave them at Polly's? Get them mixed up when the laundryman came to gather a new batch of dirty clothes? No searching through my closet, my bedroom, my bags yielded results. I was sure I'd misplaced them. They were too big, old and worn out for anyone to mistake them for their own. But no matter how long I searched, there were no underpants lying about anywhere. This was a problem. I'd have to wait weeks, more likely months, to get some from home. I asked my neighbors, talked to Polly in a quick phonecall and when everyone said, "Nope, we haven't seen your underpants," I resigned myself to making do by washing the remaining few every three days. I wrote home asking my mom, stepmom and aunt for a new supply. I'd be lucky if one of the packages made it to me before the end of my two-year stay. Afia, the kids in the compound, my laundryman all said they hadn't seen them.

Several weeks later, after I'd nearly forgotten about the missing underpants, I returned home from school pushing my mobylette into its parking spot near the small garden at my entryway. Setting the kickstand, I looked up and saw a full assortment of colorful panties hanging shamelessly on the community clothesline, drying themselves in the late day sun.

"Oh!! There they are!" I called out happily to my neighbors as I strode into the common cooking area where everyone was gathered. "I found them! My missing underpants!" How kind of someone to have retrieved them, washed them and hung them on the line. I settled into the afternoon's work and plucked those panties off the line just before sundown, smiling gratefully. I was relieved to have them back. The generosity of my compound mates continued to surprise.

I pointed out the panties to Afia and asked her if she knew anything about them. She shook her head from side to side, indicating an emphatic "*Non, Mees!*"

When my landlord returned home that day, I called out to him.

"*Oncle! Oncle! Plus de mystère! Les caleçons sont là!*" I joyfully declared that the mystery of the underpants had been solved and that someone had generously found and washed them for me.

"Très bien, Mademoiselle." He seemed pleased.

Later that evening, when darkness had invited the cricket chatter and all of us were busy with the work of washing dinner dishes, putting little ones to bed, reading or studying by kerosene lamp light, I heard shouting. I could no longer concentrate when a series of slaps and screams came from the room adjacent to my kitchen. I recognized Afia's voice. She was crying and choking on pleas to stop someone from something.

"WHAP!"

"Non, Oncle, NON!"

"Whap! WHAP!" Oncle was speaking a language I didn't understand interspersed with French. "You THIEF! You're terrible! I'm ashamed of you!"

"WHAP!"

It was a horrifying sound. I listened and grimaced as Afia couldn't catch her breath before she was struck again. I was terrified. One of the children ran up my steps, pounded on my screen door and asked me to go next door to Oncle's. I hastened to his room and saw Afia bent over, trembling and whimpering in a corner. A neighbor was sitting on a stool and an older man I'd never seen was standing next to Oncle in the dark.

"Are these your *caleçons?*" the elder asked, thrusting a pair of faded underpants in my direction.

"Oui," I paused then answered, hesitating for the correct reply to secure Afia's release from whatever was happening. Oncle Claude lunged at Afia again and resumed beating her, pieces of a stick breaking and flying

as he shouted. Afia screamed at each of the blows. Claude lost control in the dark room and the man on the stool jumped up and ran over to stop him. At his call, two older boys ran into the room and wrapped their arms around Claude to stop him from more furious beating. The girl ran out of the room sobbing. I returned to my quarters, shaken.

Confused, upset by the violence I'd witnessed and feeling terrible guilt, I tried to resume my evening activities. I heard only Afia's whimpering from the cooking area. I attempted to grade papers, wash dishes, read, but I couldn't focus on the task. I finally went to bed, distraught. My underpants had caused this. What could I do to save my girl-boy? Had she stolen my underpants? What would she steal next? Why did I have so many underpants anyway? How had I contributed to Afia's continual failure? To the belief that girls and women were less than men?

Two days later, Afia appeared at my doorstep, shaking. Head turned down so that I could only see those small curly-Qs of hair, she muttered what I assumed to be an apology and then disappeared. Before I could offer words of encouragement, add a moral to the tale, or ask her an innocent question, she was gone.

I saw her only once or twice after that in the courtyard, but she always refused to look at me. She didn't return to help in my house. Her uncle was now embarrassed in front of me as well. Fed up with Afia's troublesome mistakes, he became more severe. He declared her unemployed as my sometimes boy and increased the rigor of her duties for him. Shortly afterwards, he sent her back to her village.

I remained mystified about Afia, my role in her failure at our compound, and how she represented the fate of so many women in Togo. From my limited perspective, my students weren't like Afia. Was it privilege? Was Afia's obsequiousness learned? Innate? I asked myself questions about her for weeks after the underpants incident. Why hadn't she asked me for some underpants? Would I have denied her? Wouldn't they have just fallen down when she wore them anyway? What else had she wanted? What other things had she taken? I resolved to devote myself more seriously to educating myself and my young female students at Collège Adèle so that I could help appropriately and so that a professional life was possible for each of them. They did not deserve Afia's fate. No one did. I came to believe that Afia's failure had been systematically taught, her inability to achieve, learned. Given my naïve optimism, my innocent wish for her was powerless in the face of what she'd come to believe about herself.

The underpants in question were never very important after that. I couldn't even bring myself to wear them. I felt a mixture of guilt, shame, embarrassment, and an utter lack of cultural comprehension when I spotted them. They sat at the bottom of my bureau beside the three pairs that I did wear in my private and stubborn show of solidarity with Afia, my former girl-boy.

SOCCER MATCH

MY WEEK WAS FRAMED BY TUESDAY AND FRIDAY, the two days mail arrived. And still no letter in scratchy writing from Canada. I guessed Denis wasn't ever going to write. Or at least no letter from him was going to make it all the way to Lama-Kara. Too bad. I supposed my affection for Denis had been stronger than his attachment to me. I was so disappointed. After a flurry of letters from my dad and step-mom with upbeat, encouraging advice, there had been a sudden

With friends on an excursion

drop-off in communication. I made excuses. Letters got lost all the time. Everyone was busy. It was easy to make a mistake with my address. But lags in letters left me feeling disconnected and far, far away. After many weeks, finally, I received a letter from my stepmom with a possible explanation for the silence. In addition to an update of the misadventures of her braying beagle, she'd been to a "fat farm" to lose weight. A what?

I only lost eight pounds...figured it cost me $100 per pound...and I lost it all in my face...don't think it will last...my clothes fit better but my ghastly eating habits are creeping back...I did sneak out one night with another woman and we celebrated with a GRAND mexican dinner...got caught the next day with garlic and onions on my breath...it was a hoot and I met some marvelous friends...I really missed my refrigerator...and will never leave it again. NEVER.

I was so happy to hear from her that I forgave her kooky letter-writing style refusing to use either capital letters or periods and laughed aloud at her antics. Did she forget she was writing to an English teacher? Did she really PAY to lose weight? She missed her refrigerator? I didn't even have a refrigerator! My African friends would have had a hard time understanding someone who paid money to not eat. American ways seemed stranger and stranger. She was one kooky stepmom but boy, was I happy to be reconnected.

My mother's letters too had become less frequent. I learned that my grandfather had died and, understandably, Christmas had lacked its familiar cheerfulness. I was sad for my mom and a little sad for myself, having hoped that upon my return from Togo, maybe, just maybe, I would have been able to interest my grandfather in my life. More bad news. President Nixon was targeting the Peace Corps in a plan to cut foreign aid. Fifteen out of fifty-five countries were going to lose Peace Corps volunteers and possibly Togo was one of the targets. To make things worse, interest payments on my student loan were due.

I complained to André about the bad news, my homesickness, the isolation I felt teaching at Collège Adèle, the relentlessness of preparing lessons. He did his best to cheer me up but he also had a demanding and unpredictable work schedule. I often thought he was the one who should have been complaining, although he never did. I sometimes felt a great distance from him too, discovering that his politics were more conservative than mine. I shouldn't have been surprised, but I was.

"How can you NOT have an opinion about America's role in Vietnam? How can you be neutral about Richard Nixon?" I asked. I was self-conscious of my moodiness but couldn't seem to control it. Sometimes I felt like our cultural differences got in the way of a deeper relationship. I couldn't forget his comment about a "scheduled" wedding six months after my departure. Maybe I'd feel better when I received more letters. Maybe I'd feel better as the dust and wind of the harmattan finally subsided and we'd get some rain again.

In anticipation of a break in the heat, André encouraged me to take one Sunday off and go to a championship soccer match. I wasn't much of a sports fan and knew little about competitive soccer, but I was desperate for a break from preparing lessons and I figured I might learn something about the bewildering popularity of "foot," or *fútbol*.

From the moment they walked, boys everywhere kicked small wads of paper, cans, gourds and, if they were lucky, balls. Soccer had not been popular in the U.S. when I was younger, but I'd played kickball as a child. Perhaps I'd learn about the sport and like it. And maybe I'd run into people I knew at the match. I was feeling unusually open and carefree as I headed out.

"BANG!!" The screen door slammed shut behind me. I stepped across the smooth cement stoop onto the hard earth of the courtyard. The air felt humid, almost heavy, as I strode past the large Mimosa tree, the only shade in the shared space of our compound. A few scrawny chickens clucked and darted away from my step. Two children played with sticks gathered for cooking the evening meal. I greeted their mama, my neighbor, with a routine "*Alafia-we?*" and walked out onto the road that led to the field. There were white billowy clouds overhead. They screened the sun's brightness and would've been a relief except for the terrible heaviness about the air. I was sure that harmattan had ended. I tried to feel reassured and picked up my stride with the certainty that rain would arrive within the hour.

The promise of showers and finding myself outside the compound on a deserted Sunday afternoon swelled my lightheartedness. The hint of rain in sub-Saharan Africa, a heady mixture of moisture and dust, often quick to become water and mud, is a scent one does not easily forget. There is often a drop in temperature and a welcome shading of the sun's brightness. But what lingers is the deep, rich, metallic smell that brings with it release and relief. Anticipating a sudden storm, I made my way to the soccer match through heavy air under auspicious clouds with fresh energy.

A series of twisting paths took me around walled compounds through sparsely wooded groves. I passed two women carrying bulbous water jugs on their heads and a pack of skinny, scruffy-looking dogs growling at each other, competing for edible scraps atop a roadside garbage mound. Otherwise, the path was unusually empty. I heard the noise of cheering fans long before I reached the field. The game was being held at an open, grassy expanse used for community gatherings year-round. It was bordered on one side by teak trees and on another by whitewashed school buildings. As I arrived, I spotted more people than I could easily count standing around the edge of the field, and clusters of young children running about behind them. Except for these young children, everyone was absorbed in the match, well underway. Spectators were shouting and gesturing wildly at the players.

I saw André, caught up in lively conversation with some uniformed *militaires*. The humidity had intensified and I observed people removing pieces of clothing, putting them to use as towels to wipe streams of sweat or hats to shade the sun. Some used shirts as African-style pom-poms and swung them victoriously if a play was good or threateningly if a play was bad. I approached the sideline, signaled a brief greeting to André, and shifted my focus from the spectators to the game. A forward passed the ball with a graceful swipe of his bare foot. The players wore only shorts of many different patterns and colors. Aside from following the direction of a kicked ball, there were no clues to match player and team. Teammates ran around the field, communicating to each other through facial expressions and sudden commands I couldn't understand. Their dark brown bodies glistened with perspiration. Whenever a player kicked or jumped, there was a little burst of spray, a shout from the crowd and colorful clothes thrust skyward.

It was hard for me to keep up with the constant back-and-forth of the match. The crowd echoed its intensity. Spectators seemed angry and on edge. They batted children away, tussled with each other over space near the field, and shouted menacingly when one team made an error, a poor play or missed a goal. I couldn't help but think the weather had stretched everyone's tolerance for friendly competition just a bit too far. My students had been talking of this match for weeks. They said that the game was pivotal and they'd been claiming their favorite team's imminent victory with a passion I found amusing. I wished they'd been as interested in memorizing the weekly rhyme in English class as they were in the soccer match. Nonetheless, I recognized its importance and was glad I'd come to the game. I was trying to be part of my community, I reminded myself. The few stores that were normally open on Sundays had closed so that patrons and their families could also attend. This match was a big deal.

After several frustrated attempts, one team finally scored a goal and the crowd erupted in a deafening roar. The noise of fans subsided, play got underway again, and then a whistle blew for half time. A few familiar students and their friends approached me. I tried to appear more comfortable than I really was. I didn't understand the subtleties of this game or why everyone took it so seriously. What <u>was</u> it about soccer? Could I fit in without being a fan? Without understanding the game?

"*Bonjour Mees! Bonjour Mees! Qu'est-ce vous pensez du match? Vous aimez le fútbol? C'est très bon, n'est-ce pas??*" I smiled, greeted the students, fanning myself with my hand and directed our exchange away from football to the weather.

"*Ouf! Qu'il fait chaud!*" I replied, complaining about the heat and announcing that I was waiting for rain. "*J'attends la pluie.*" The young people surrounded me and in noisy unison protested my wish for rain. They were anxious to witness the outcome of the match. A sudden downpour would delay this.

Above the voices of the students, I became aware of a sudden commotion at the far end of the field. There was shouting, a loud thud and the bleat of a wounded animal. I heard more noise: a mixture of cheers, jeers, shrieks. In the middle of a handshake, I looked over to see a near-starved dog flung into the air by a kick, the same swift kick I'd seen on the playing field. This time, however, fans were joining in the play. Fans and militaires. Two young men ran to the dog as he fell at their feet and together they beat him in the ribs with sticks. It became a free-for-all, supporters of two soccer teams, soldiers, policemen and family members united against a meandering, scruffy-looking dog who'd wandered onto the field at half-time, scrounging for food scraps spectators might have left behind. Opponents a few minutes ago, enthusiasts of the two teams acted together. Everyone near the scene, young and old, player, policeman and spectator, joined in the dog's destruction. They kicked it, beat it with sticks, and pelted it with rocks until the frightened yelps stopped and the dog lay dead on the field.

I watched from a distance, aghast, and suddenly felt sick to my stomach. I noted that André had stayed on the sidelines and watched too. I was relieved he hadn't participated in the brutality. The people around me started laughing and slapped each other with amusement. My skin felt cold. Laughing? They must be embarrassed. They couldn't really take delight in such savagery, could they? I heard the scraping of dry leaves and branches as the dog's body was tossed beyond the teak trees and the hollow "whump" it made as it hit the ground. I backed away from my students and other spectators, trying to hide my horror as the match resumed. I couldn't stay or gather the wherewithal to mutter a quick good-bye as I stepped away, picking up speed as I gained distance. The drama of the innocent dog played over and over in my mind as I practically ran home, not seeing very clearly, hoping I could find my way.

I was still shaking when I arrived home. I poured myself several cups of water and set to washing the morning's dishes in order to calm down. When André showed up about an hour later, I asked what had happened. He laughed. He couldn't understand why I'd left before the match was over or why I'd been so shocked and put off by the dog incident. I was stunned by his reaction and his lack of sympathy for the dog. I couldn't understand such cruelty, such pleasure in killing an innocent animal. I didn't learn which team, in the end, had won the game. I didn't care. In fact, I vowed to not ever attend another soccer game.

Throughout the following week I heard my students talk about the incident, huddled in groups before and after class. They winced and squealed, unable to contain a kind of delight in telling and retelling the tale. I tried not to listen. I did my best to understand how kind, friendly people could laugh at such callous behavior. Throughout the next few weeks, when American friends stopped by to visit or passed through town, I told them about the dog incident. Some said that it was just the poor dog's bad luck, that Togolese chased dogs away all the time and the intensity of the soccer game had made people unusually brutish. Others believed such sadistic behavior was due to the pervasiveness of witchcraft. I thought of what I'd come across in some of the villages I'd visited: small statues smeared with blood and dolls in the market covered with nails. From time to time I'd met a villager walking alone covered in layers of dirty white cloth wielding wooden bludgeons or twirling and chanting eerie melodies. I knew these were signs of voodoo and since I'd been taught not to ask questions or in any way challenge practices I didn't understand, I'd kept quiet. Had the soccer match incident been a result of witchcraft? Did people believe that the dog had been sent onto the field to jinx one of the teams?

André never said anything more about it. Perhaps it was his way of not stirring conflict. And surely he knew more than he was willing to share. I didn't ask. I also realized that the clouds that had so assuredly presaged rain on the day of the match had failed to fulfill their promise. I couldn't stop suffering for the dog.

At night, Ewart dreamed of Africa.

—**JULIAN SMITH**, *Crossing the Heart of Africa:
An Odyssey of Love and Adventure*

MOVING OUT & BEYOND

FOCUSED ON LESSON PLANS and letters home as a way of moving beyond my blunders with Afia and the memory of the soccer match. Recurring nightmares of Afia's beating and the fate of the innocent dog forced me to reconsider long-held cultural values. Could actions be right for one group and wrong for another? Were there absolute rules that <u>everyone</u> ought to follow across time periods and cultures? Where did one stretch and shrink respect, tolerance even, for such radically differ-

With Rudy and Pam on the Nice beach

ent approaches to life? Didn't a successful adjustment to one new culture prepare you for others? I believed I had a firm grasp of these issues, but recent incidents had tapped vulnerabilities and prompted unexpected questions. Adjusting successfully to one set of values didn't necessarily prepare us for another. I retreated slightly from my commitment to "community integration," doing as the locals did, and took refuge in my reading and sewing and bead bracelets.

Always with a preoccupation on my teaching, I added tongue-twisters to Friday's fun list and continued to teach a new song each week if everyone had paid attention in class. I demonstrated exaggerated mouth positions to help students pronounce initial sounds in "Fuzzy Wuzzy" and "Woodchuck," watching as they stumbled over consonant blends or accented the wrong syllables. They'd collapse in laughter and slap each other on the shoulder, feeling so silly.

"Not so loud!" I warned them. "Don't let la Soeur Directrice hear us. We'll have to go back to our chapter review if we're too noisy." They quieted down right away. Between lesson prep, test design and corrections, I plotted a playful summer getaway. Maybe out of Togo, even out of Africa. Three childhood friends were traveling separately from California to Europe. I wrote letters to them, proposing a reunion, hatching a dream. I fantasized about getting together, but details like enough money and a practical meet-up location convinced me that it would be tricky to pull off. Communication was slow and unpredictable. Where would I stay? How would I make arrangements?

I'd never travelled on my own internationally or been to Europe, so I waited for signs of a manageable scheme. While waiting, I continued to make good on resolutions to become a better teacher, a better dancer, a more supportive friend to Polly, a more frequent correspondent to everyone at home, and less of a whiner with André. I avoided topics where I knew we might not agree and cast aside fears that our relationship was becoming superficial. When others asked, I claimed to be well adjusted, settled in and happy. The end of my first year in northern Togo was approaching. I had learned to move easily through days without running water or electricity. I could eat spicy stew with my hands and not burn either my fingers from the heat or my mouth from the spice. I could savor a calabash shower. I took great pleasure in these accomplishments, and admitted that with a few exceptions like male attitudes towards women and general treatment of animals, I fit right in to my community and mostly lived like a privileged Togolese. I'd studied new languages, tried to live according to a more relaxed sense of time, improved my guitar playing, successfully negotiated relationships according to varied cultural prescriptions, struggled through a year of a job where the work was never done, and worked alongside intimidating colleagues.

When letters dribbled in from my American pals agreeing to a European rendezvous, I counted what I'd saved from my monthly salary of $150 and realized I didn't have enough money to fly to Europe. My dad and stepmom wired $150 and a telegram announced that my oldest friend would be in Nice taking a language course about the same time I could travel. I decided that I'd earned a vacation!

So I sketched out a trip to Europe on a very tight budget, setting up a series of stops along the Côte d'Azur, following a route that hugged the Mediterranean, making my way from Madrid to Rome. Two of the nuns at Collège Adèle offered me low-cost hospitality at convents in both the starting and ending points, bookending an otherwise secular adventure with spiritual anchors. The vacation made sense. I'd find comfort in the familiarity of western cultures. I reasoned that the Ghana adventure had helped me appreciate Togo. Maybe something like this would happen again by visiting Europe. I'd also get to spend time with at least one old friend. I'd return balanced between east and west, prepared for a productive second school year.

Peace Corps encouraged us to travel between teaching terms, but required that we complete a summer service project contributing to our jobs or our communities. Some volunteers built new latrines, taught English to village children or helped improve public water wells. I decided to compile a small booklet of children's rhymes and folksongs I'd used to teach English grammar and enliven my classes. I'd pass it on as a gift to other English teachers in Togo. So at school year's end, I spent several days in Lomé beginning my project by making a list of songs and rhymes I wanted to include. Then, through offers of my famous homemade mango compôte, I cajoled Brian, a school construction volunteer and a clever cartoonist, into producing a series of illustrations to accompany the songs. The result was a whimsical and entertaining collection. There was a smug Michael rowing the boat ashore, a tightly clustered group of saints with oversized African sandals marching in, and some haughty blackbirds sitting on a hill. I completed the Table of Contents and assembled the nearly forty pages. Then I got ready to take off for Europe, my first international adventure all by myself.

I flew to Madrid and made my way to my colleague Sister Lorenca's home convent. I liked this Spanish nun from Collège Adèle very much. She smiled often and her French was animated, even friendly. Because she would be there on vacation too, I looked forward to getting to know her better. But as I moved into the convent, it didn't seem likely that I'd be spending time with her. The building was vast, with broad ochre hallways that were empty and silent. The few people I encountered walked past me lost in thought or engaged in soft conversation with someone else. At my first evening meal in the cavernous dining hall I was eager to make friends and greet the nun serving everyone. Sister Lorenca wasn't among my dining mates.

"Good evening, Sister!"

She whispered back, "Hello," and without a pause or a smile continued spooning out soup, the folds of her robe's long sleeves sweeping the smooth dark table as she moved from one person to the next. I sat in an uncomfortable straight-backed chair, trying to exchange a friendly nod or a brief greeting with one of the other diners, all of whom were nuns clad entirely in all white or all black. We chewed without talking. I looked everywhere for behavior cues, trying hard to follow rules that hadn't been explained. I learned to speak softly, cast my eyes downward, and tried to memorize the circuitous route from dining hall to my small, sparse and windowless room. Entering my cell, I always found the darkness a bit unsettling. The retreat-like setting should have been refreshing after the noise and crowds and activity in Togo, but it felt lonely and unhappy. I should have been savoring the privacy after many months of having none, but I felt completely out of place. I became somber, padding softly through the hallways just like everyone else. I survived the silent meal ritual and spent evening hours in bed, staring at the ceiling and wondering about the life of a nun. I felt so isolated. Sister Lorenca was nowhere to be found. During the day, I walked the city streets noticing the speeding cars, the plentiful magazine stands and people walking everywhere. The women with long dark hair and bright red lipstick stood out in the crowds. I was struck by the array of food, such a contrast to what I was used to. Watermelons, peaches, donuts, cheese, lettuce. This was such a different world, I remarked, beginning my comparisons to Togo. On the third morning, I slipped out of the convent and caught a train for Nice. I spotted Sister Lorenca as she was leaving too, to visit her family in the Pyrenees.

"Dommage qu'on n'était pas ensemble," I told her, disappointed that we hadn't been able to spend time together. Hadn't she wanted to get to know me too? Although grateful to have had a place to stay in Madrid, I was relieved to end my stay at the convent and returned to speaking more naturally and moving more spontaneously. We waved goodbye to each other as we promised to spend more time together when we returned to Togo. I was surprised that she'd been friendlier in Togo than in her native country.

After my traveling experiences in Togo and Ghana, the train ride along the coast was fun, smooth and efficient. I reveled in taking an assigned seat, departing and arriving on time. It was much less colorful and less entertaining, but so much more predictable. I took heart in my ability to manage such different transportation systems somewhat successfully. The truth is I was blown away by the contrasts. Just as the schedule had promised, I disembarked on time in Nice to an explosion of color and movement. Walking from the train station, I again passed bright yellow, red, orange fruits and vegetables on display, leafy green plants and bushes lining the streets and sidewalks, and silver white beaches. This color palette was set against blue skies and broad grey streets. There was a shiny brilliance about the Mediterranean light, so unlike the earthy reds, browns and deep greens of Africa.

People moved differently too. They walked, worked, drove, and talked in street-corner clusters, along the Quaie de Nice and at the water's edge. Children playing? Shifting my bags from one shoulder to another, I noticed children frolicking on the beach and stopped to watch. In Togo I rarely saw children playing—there was too much work for them to do. Suspended between shock and delight, I caught myself staring at adults, strolling, sipping, reading, lounging. What a contrast these sights were to my short stay in the convent and my first year in Lama-Kara.

Expecting to feel at home, I was confused. Who was I? Where did I come from? It was ridiculous feeling so muddled. I undoubtedly looked American. The hair, the clothes, the walk were a sure give-away, although I was often mistaken for Dutch or Danish. Yet I claimed allegiance to Africa, identifying most with the continent I'd recently gotten to know. Crazy! My cultural identity and loyalty had shifted. I was drawn to Africans whenever I saw them and many were scattered along the Mediterranean coast, most having miraculously made it across the Sahara and then the salty sea to tend parking lots, sweep streets, study or sell bags on the sidewalks. I wondered how they managed, negotiating the pace, people and lifestyle of this radically different place. I felt a newfound sympathy for these visible foreigners and could relate to their feelings of displacement. One balmy evening, shortly after my arrival in Nice, I met a man in a small convenience shop who said he was from Togo.

"Togo??!! Mais moi aussi, je suis de Togo!!" I jumped at this opportunity to announce that I was from Togo too. Then and there, between the bottled juices and containers of yogurt, I learned that Rudy had been in southern France for a number of years and was currently working the night shift for a local high-end hotel. He wasn't exactly happy living

in Europe, he confessed, as we moved to the cheese section, ignoring the smells and making way for other busy customers. He told me he'd learned to survive, perhaps even prosper, by African standards. An expert at clucking disapproval *à la français*, and pursing his lips as he paused between crisp Parisian French phrases, Rudy invited me to stay in his small apartment during my visit to Nice. Typical African generosity! Our opposite schedules worked well as I'd be out during the day when he needed to sleep. Wary at first that staying at his place would involve more than just friendly gratitude, I considered the alternative of a crowded hostel full of ragtag international travelers where I'd been for the previous two nights.

"Mais toi-la, viens chez moi!" he insisted, assuring me that romance, or at least sex, was not part of the agreement. So I accepted his offer, loving the idea of coming and going as I wished. I cheerfully carried my two small bags to Rudy's and stashed them in a corner.

Through conversations at odd hours of the day, crossing paths at dawn or dusk, Rudy and I developed a friendship. He was the paternal figure lecturing me, the confused and curious traveler, on the deep differences and successful navigation strategies between European and African values and lifestyles. I loved his protective attention and did my best to feel at home inside his tiny apartment of dark maroon drapes, carpeting and upholstery. Like my convent room, there was little light in this small space. Rudy kept the curtains closed in order to sleep in the daytime. Everything smelled of stale oil from many nights of his home-cooked peanut sauce. So it was refreshing to step outside the apartment, into the bright, sunny streets of Nice, momentarily escaping the deepening disorientation I felt when I remembered I'd come from

Africa. Always aiming to fit in was problematic during my constant relocating.

One afternoon I strode out of the apartment building to meet up with my childhood friend Pam. She had arrived in Nice before me and had found the last bed in a small hostel not far from Rudy's apartment. We were inseparable during our time in Nice. It was so comforting to be with her. Our reunion seemed too good to be true. La Côte d'Azur seemed the perfect setting for such a magical encounter as we each struggled with difficult personal issues. I was in deep culture shock—trying every day to understand who I was exactly, African? American? *Niçoise?* I felt suspended in confusion and guilt about being on vacation and wondering how my life in Togo fit into larger life goals. I wondered if my "community integration" training been too effective. Was I not able to accommodate several different cultures simultaneously? Just who was I? I couldn't get used to children laughing and playing with each other, men and women lounging, sipping wine, doing little more than enjoying themselves. I gasped when entering even the simplest grocery stores stacked with an array of so much more merchandise than even the best market in Togo. And frankly, though I considered myself nearly fluent in French by now, the accent and speed of the version spoken in Nice was tricky. It skipped over significant consonants and made me feel helpless when I should've been masterful, rolling easily from understanding to responding. The language had often been my anchor in Togo, the one buoy I'd held to as an outsider, but the variety of French here had me feeling adrift.

Pam's struggle was more straightforward, to me at least. Her father had passed away the previous spring when she'd been preparing to depart on this long-awaited study-trip to Europe. After initial approval, Pam's mom was suddenly demanding that she return home. As daughter and only child, Pam was trying to sort out her responsibilities to the legacy of her father, to her mother's unexpected request, and to balance her own desire to complete the language course. She resisted the pull to go home. "I wish I knew what to do," she muttered over and over. "I can't think of anything I can do for my mother now if I go home." Stay here! Stay with me! I couldn't be objective. I wanted Pam to stay in southern France for at least as long as I was around. I saw how happy she was to be making progress in French and enjoying newfound friends.

"Can't you stay until the end of your language course?" I pleaded. She shrugged with indecision.

We spent afternoons strolling along the Quaie de Nice sharing our confusion and conflicting tugs, trying to decide what was right, what we wanted, what was possible. I felt an uncharacteristic calm, a steadiness with my old friend. And I appreciated how her dilemma distracted me from my own. We practiced colloquial French, the *Nicoise* version, shared critical reviews of several versions of *Salade Niçoise*, and wondered how in the world people on the beach were able to change their clothes and bare their bodies before the whole world. We savored gourmet leftovers Rudy brought us from his hotel restaurant, and we made friends with local artists who invited us to a street market and gifted us beautiful batik silk scarves. We got free tickets to a performance of *Hair*, in French of course, and delighted at how much of the lyrics we could understand. In spite of the struggles, our time together was heartwarming. After many nights' tossing and turning, Pam decided to return to the States, realizing that being closer to home would comfort her mother. When Pam left, Rudy made his move.

"*Tu es belle, tu sais. Amusons-nous avant ton départ!*" I was pretty, he said, and proposed a quick affair before I left Nice. Every time we met after that he pulled me toward him, wrapping his arms around my shoulders as I wriggled out of his hold. I reminded him of his initial pledge, but he didn't pay attention, so I got ready to leave too. Rudy didn't take my rebuffs personally, cheerfully escorting me to the train station and making sure I knew where to wait and what to pay. I would miss his kindness.

My brief stay in Rome was full of tourist sites. Marble steps, ancient statues, sunny days. I stayed in a convent that was more like an inexpensive guesthouse and missed connections to new and old friends. Peace Corps' emphasis on fitting in with the community, acting as if I were a local, had made me a terrible tourist. So after visiting the most famous spots, I longed to return to Togo where I could claim to be part of a familiar community. Before leaving Rome I decided to try a phone call home, a feat nearly impossible from Lama-Kara. In a wood-paneled public phone booth at the post office, I waited for nearly an hour to connect to my mom.

"Mom?! Mom! It's me calling from Rome! Hi! How are you?!"

"Mere?! Huh?! Hello?" She sounded remote, confused. I explained that I'd been trying to reach her and the line had been busy for a long time. For an hour she was talking on the phone?!

"How's everything in Lama-Kara?" she asked, words all running together.

"I'm in Rome, Mom, at the end of my vacation in Europe!"

"Oh, that's right. You met Pam. Hot diggedy! Do you need money? I'll send you money. How much?" There were long pauses between words now. Was it the connection? Was there an echo? And her language was definitely slurred. I immediately determined she'd been drinking, replying that I didn't need money and was no longer interested in talking. We exchanged a few more empty greetings before I told her I had to say goodbye. I paid for the call and walked out of the crowded post office deeply disappointed. I thought her drinking had subsided, that she'd been doing so well. I'd heard that she was exercising, engaged in her own teaching and looking forward to the upcoming school year. What a setback this was.

On the airplane headed back to Africa, I reflected on my brief European vacation and tried to focus on the positive aspects of the journey, although worry about my mom weighed me down. I'd made a Togolese friend in Europe, Pam and I had regained our childhood closeness, and I'd gotten a welcome break from teaching. Was I ready to return? Oh yes! I arrived in Togo happy to have traveled, but happier to be back.

In Lomé I was greeted by the familiar sounds and smells that had once been so hard to bear. What had been a shock to my senses a year before and what had rattled my twenty-two-year-old sense of normal was no longer rattling. I could meet the familiar with poise, feeling unchallenged and prepared. I settled temporarily into another volunteer's house, enjoying running water, electricity and a comfortable room to complete my songbook project before the school year began. It felt slightly uncomfortable, appreciating this level of living ease. I wasn't used to the conveniences of the modern house and felt guilty enjoying them. Was this "fitting it"? Perhaps in Lomé, where the living was easier, it was. But these creature comforts balanced the hard work I was doing.

Each morning I headed to a dingy room in the Peace Corps office, catching up with staff members I adored, and plotting out pages of my booklet by placing words and drawings. It was August and the post

Cover of my songbook

rainy season humidity of equatorial Africa bore down, a stream of sweat running down my spine as I pressed sticky keys on a manual typewriter, punching letters into stencil film that smelled inky and oozed small bursts of liquid purple. With a fine-pointed pen, I traced over the lines of each of Brian's playful cartoon scenes, careful not to lose the angle of a crow's eyebrow or the nonchalant smile of a saint at the front of the pack. I worked on layout and organization, cutting and placing text and cartoons according to teaching points they highlighted. The resulting booklet had a lively, whimsical feel to it.

"Look at my book!" I tracked down Christian in the Peace Corps office.

"*Mais Mademoiselle*," his eyes smiled. "*Vous êtes auteur.*"

"An author, Christian? *Non, non,* but a much better teacher than I was a year ago." He nodded in approval. This early effort at producing a book was immensely satisfying, and seemed the perfect transition from my first year of teaching to a new, second year. Once the book was ready to copy, I enjoyed luxurious afternoons in Lomé playing tennis, going to the market and getting together with other volunteers returning from their summer travels. I couldn't believe my good fortune at having been able to travel to Europe while indulging what I considered luxury living upon my return to Togo. Perhaps I'd managed a healthy balance between my pledge to live like a local while acknowledging my western roots.

> I started to get up to pack my backpack and was stunned to discover that I could not stand...I stood up and sat down again three times in rapid succession, my legs folding beneath me like a marionette. The dizziness in my head was so severe that palm trees, ocean, clothesline zoomed by me as if on a high-speed carousel.
>
> —**TANYA SHAFFER**, *Somebody's Heart is Burning: A Woman Wanderer in Africa*

DISEQUILIBRIUM

IN LOMÉ, I HAPPILY RECONNECTED with friends and pretended that a visit to Europe and daily life in a western culture had been seamless. But it hadn't. I'd bombarded myself with comparisons to "the way it was in Togo" and was shocked and set off balance by sights and sensations that had been so familiar *Before Africa*. Now, after nearly a month on the road and away from my home in Lama-Kara, I was anxious to return to my job, my house, and my friends in the north, especially André. I looked forward to a lighter teaching schedule for my second year at Collège Adèle: fewer levels of English and an art or PE class. It would be so much easier. In Lomé, I reflected on my midpoint as a Peace Corps volunteer and wrote in a letter to my dad that I felt refreshed and even excited about getting back to work. I described my move to a new compound with increased privacy and a better latrine. But even in my enthusiasm, I felt strangely exhausted. This wasn't jetlag. My limbs were heavy, my mind muddled, my head ached. In fact, with each day I felt weaker, and when I asked Peace Corps Nurse Edith if I should see the doctor, she said that Peace Corps Togo doctors were transitioning, from old doc to new doc, and that I was probably coming down with a good stiff case of the flu.

"Take two aspirin every four hours," she advised. "Get plenty of rest and you'll shake this soon." I did everything Edith recommended and continued to feel increasingly weak, heavier, groggier, less able to move. I languished in Lomé at the volunteer's house where I was staying, trying to read or eat or chat with friends, but everything took more effort than I could muster. I was so relieved to be able to stay in this house where creature comforts were plentiful.

When Polly returned from her summer break, I backed out of a provisions run and stayed at home in bed while she shopped. I lost my appetite, stopped working on the songbook, or reading the books I hadn't finished in Europe, discovering that I couldn't sit up for the amount of time letter-writing required. Polly sat at my bedside telling me of her summer adventures and looking concerned that my flu symptoms lingered. Still, I believed that I was getting better every day. In denial, I wrote a letter home:

> Here I am, Mom, with this poor overdue letter! I've been sick and have been in bed for nearly 2 weeks. It was some mysterious virus. Miserable, really. I've lost <u>lots</u> of weight. My friends hardly recognize me. My appetite is coming back slowly. I'm still weak and tired, but taking it easy. I'm just thanking God it's finished—<u>me</u> in <u>bed</u> in Lomé is no easy prospect!! It's always good I can't write you til <u>after</u> it's over so as not to worry you! I'm not heading north 'til I'm <u>really</u> feeling good—probably this Sunday...

In spite of the optimistic report to my mom, by the end of the second week of feeling crummy, veins protruded from my wrist and my nails were blue. I felt my hip bones and thought of the cows I saw often in northern Togo, ambling listlessly from one parched patch of dried earth to another, shoulder blades and hip bones holding up dull, drooping skin. All I wanted to do was sleep. And then I began to have sudden hot flashes followed by icy cold chills. Talking took too much energy and the possibility that I'd never be well again flashed in and out of wakeful moments. I had really weird dreams. Some were vivid flashbacks of traveling in Europe; others were long interrupted conversations with my mother on the telephone. Most were echoes of bedside chats with Polly, replayed in distorted voices with words omitted and all meaning lost. I was hallucinating.

Had I paid closer attention to the thorough health lectures Peace Corps laid out for us at the beginning, had I heeded the telltale warning signs, had I been more attuned to my physical state, I would have known that it was not the flu I had, but malaria. Edith dismissed my medical symptoms and had picked up on my fragile emotional state. She'd labeled it Culture Shock. "You have a weak immune system because you're an emotional wreck," she declared. "As soon as you realize you're back in Togo, you'll get over it." She was partly right. I was feeling particularly confused and vulnerable. But I was also seriously ill. My red blood cells, as well as my sense of what was "normal", were under siege. Edith reappeared now, two weeks after her first diagnosis, flanked by a new Peace Corps doctor "fresh off the plane", who immediately recognized my condition as malarial. He mobilized on the spot by giving me a huge shot of quinine, preparing a supply of blood in case I needed an immediate transfusion, and scheduled the two of us on the first flight out of Lomé headed for the American military hospital in Frankfurt, Germany. Polly started praying and Peace Corps notified my mother.

The new doc considered my case so urgent he didn't unpack his bags before he was on our Germany-bound airplane. The transition from bed to airplane was a fog. I sat shivering, my head bobbing with delirium. New doc watched my every move and tried to engage me in conversation, but I drifted in and out of focus and sleep. Fortunately, I didn't need a mid-flight blood transfusion. Dr. Singer's swift assessment of my condition and the quinine shot had already taken effect. The proliferation of white cells had been curtailed.

Hours later I woke up in a room all by myself. It was a miracle! I could lift my upper body off the bed without an excruciating headache and I could clearly hear the bustle of nurses and doors opening and closing. A medical assistant walked through the door and entered my room, telling me I was in the American Military Hospital in Frankfurt, Germany. I vaguely recalled being told this earlier, but now I was alert and could make sense of it. Woohoo! I began to stay awake for two and three hours straight, and got through a whole conversation with an attendant without wanting to sleep again. I was beginning to feel better! I couldn't believe it! Three male nurses kept bopping into my room and appeared particularly attentive to my improving condition. This bolstered my attitude as much as my increasing strength did. Soon they were walking me from one end of the hallway to the other.

"Whoopee!" I called as I spotted Private Henderson coming to escort me. "Let's go all the way to the cafeteria today! Let's go find some chocolate candy! I want to walk outside and feel the Frankfurt air! Whoopeee!! I'm well!"

A friend in front of the American Hospital in Frankfurt

By the second week in the hospital, clearly on my way to recovery, I could walk freely to the occupational therapy unit on my floor where I completed craft projects and joked with the American nurses. I rejoiced at feeling strong and having a clear head. I wanted to jump and dance and sing and shout to celebrate my recovery. I loved speaking English. When I wasn't chatting to nurses, I wondered about André. It had been so long since we talked.

It became clear that the worst was over and I schemed with the male nurses to explore corners of the hospital I hadn't been allowed to visit, and even masterminded a hospital escape to the Frankfurt Zoo. It was the material of movie scripts: tiptoeing down the back staircase to the idling Volkswagen, cruising around Frankfurt in the early fall as leaves were changing colors and the weather was getting crisp, driving through the expansive rolling fields of the zoo, lush and green, spotting giraffes and wildebeest in the distance. All of this was under the supervision of three capable and caring nurses who spoke nonstop colloquial English. Although anxious about what I was missing as the school year got underway in distant northern Togo, I figured I was lucky to be getting well so swiftly. And since my first tour of Europe hadn't included Germany, my second trip did. The chill in the air, the English language surrounding me, the attention of American men propelled me to a state of physical and mental well-being I hadn't felt in months. After a second three weeks in Europe, I returned to Togo really ready to teach.

Naturally, Peace Corps was concerned that I give myself enough time to recover from the malaria, so I was detained two more endless weeks in Lomé. School had long since begun and all my pals had returned to their posts. More restless than ever, I finally managed to convince Peace Corps staff that I was fully recovered, and was driven to Lama-Kara where I discovered that the nuns had finalized the teaching assignments, and they weren't in my favor.

Seven preps? Really?! My schedule for Year 2 was heavy. In addition to all four levels of English (which I was promised wouldn't be repeated), I was assigned to teach Art, PE and West African History.

"*Mais histoire, ma soeur? Quand je ne connais presque pas les mots pour enseigner?*" I begged la Soeur Directrice to consider the limitation of both my French and my background in history when she told me I'd be teaching West African history.

"*Voilà, Mademoiselle,*" la Directrice replied, handing me the history textbook. "*Tout est ici*—everting heah!" To her, everything was contained in the lines of a textbook. I took the book with a nod and resigned myself to a second year of hard work. I accepted the challenge, believing that the exercise would educate me in many ways. For one, I would learn about the origin of Sundia, my cat's name, I would undoubtedly get to know my students better, and my French would be magnificent. Maybe it was some form of atonement for the happy naïvete of my first year. Words from the Peace Corps invitation letter (which I appeared to have memorized) continued to rattle in my head: "You must be willing to learn as well as teach."

Even though it began more than a month late, I gratefully jumped into the school year with optimism and energy. The recurring memory of my malarial hallucinations, the two trips to Europe and the effects of the quinine shot propelled me forward. I resolved to take much better care of my health and do what I could to educate my students, these privileged West African women. I felt grateful to be alive under this warm African sun.

BALANCING ACT

SHORTLY AFTER MY RETURN TO LAMA-KARA, I lay in bed beyond the day's first light listening to the morning's accelerating momentum: the musical chatter of women greeting each other, the splashes of water poured into and out of large basins, the crackling of fires and a distant rooster crowing. The air already felt warm and I could smell the earth through the open windows in my bedroom. I looked up, beyond the mosquito net, and spotted two lizards on the ceiling. One darted forward, then back. The other did pushups with its short forelegs.

My gaze drifted to the glint of the *balançoir* I'd purchased in Lomé right before heading north from my recent recuperation. It was a crude two-piece metal sculpture. The base consisted of three levels of lean human figures, each sitting on one knee and collectively holding up two other figures with extended arms. The top two figures elevated a higher fellow who held aloft a large round disk with both arms. The very top piece, delicately balanced (thus its name balançoir, meaning swing), was another crude skinny figure with outstretched arms holding up a long arched wire weighted at each end. The top man swung gently back and forth, bending and bobbing forward and sideways with surprising grace. He never fell off his center, never tumbled from his disk. I was captivated by the interdependence of the figures and the resilience and playfulness of this simple sculpture. If only I could manage my life, its delights and disturbances, so easily, without losing my "center."

I'd moved to my new home outside of town. Neighbors and friends had helped me spruce it up by applying a thin coat of whitewash to the interior walls. We'd spread a fresh layer of cement on a section of floor that was crumbling. My new home was a significant upgrade. The compound was enclosed by thick yellow walls and the privacy they offered was an unimaginable luxury. I always had water! A well in the center of the court-yard eliminated the need to send one of the children to the river at dawn. Two latrines in the far corner provided much greater seclusion than my experience with The Throne. Sure, there were nightly cockroach raids, but cockroaches were everywhere in all sizes and everything else seemed so much more comfortable. How lucky I was! The shower stall was shaded by a leafy *bananier*, a banana tree, and I was creating a brand new flowerbed in front of the entry steps. My new neighbors were friendly and helpful. Each morning I looked out at a glorious blue sky behind puffy white clouds instead of an abandoned marketplace or dusty millet field. I was even ready to conduct interviews for a new boy. What a fascinating balancing act, I thought to myself. Weighing the comforts and the inconveniences, the work and the play, the dangers and rewards, and where I found myself now, I was excited about the future. Everything was looking up.

I thought about my return to Lama-Kara, my teaching, and how the days had been full of happy reunions and relief. I'd pulled through an advanced case of malaria. I felt healthy now, strong and proud and positive. I knew that the weather would come in extremes, that time was fluid and that ancestors were remembered and honored through daily tributes of local brew. I'd learned that there were great stretches of time

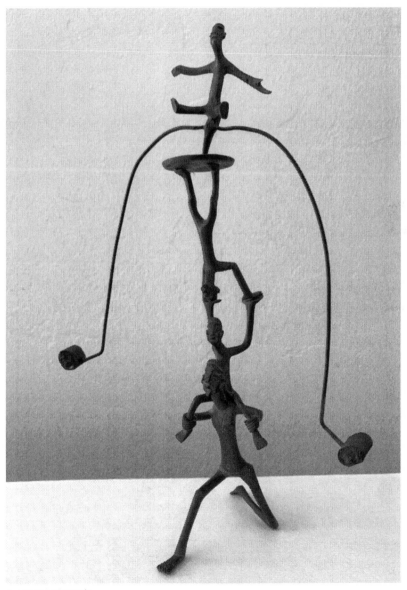

A small balançoir

that appeared without warning, hours with nothing urgent to fill them. There were also quirky problems that appeared and needed to be solved. It took a full year to <u>really</u> adjust, I reflected. I thought about my longing for friends and family back home, my joy at sending and receiving letters, the attempt to bridge the distance through the phone call home from Rome and how that had set off another short period of difficult communication with my mother.

"I'm sorry I thought you'd been drinking," I wrote after my return in a letter of apology. "You sounded so out of it. I sounded annoyed because I'd been trying for an hour to reach you. I had no idea you'd tripped over the dog and bumped your head. And I haven't written because I was adjusting to being in Lama-Kara again, not because I was mad at you!"

Reassured that she insisted she hadn't been drinking, I still wondered why she'd tripped. I took her at her word because I wanted desperately to believe her, but I wished it weren't so difficult. We began to exchange cassette tapes now in addition to letters and hearing each other's voice helped to reduce the distance between us. Mom sounded her upbeat self and I continued my struggle to believe she was sober.

Now I could mostly balance public and private time. I could also politely deflect men who continued to approach me and test my loyalty to André who'd been re-assigned from my town to a village thirty minutes south and now lived further away. I thought these men were being devious. André and I made a plan for me to visit his new home the first weekend he was free.

"*Bubu!*" we chorused, reunited after our separation. Clinging to his strong forearm with both hands, I felt anchored and safe next to him. The last few weeks had been so full of crises, changes, travel, and emotional and physical *déplacements*, that I'd lost track of how I'd missed this beautiful, kind, loving man.

"*En forme maintenant?*" he asked, seeking reassurance that I was healthy.

"*En forme! Encore plus forte que jamais!*" I told him, claiming to be stronger and healthier than ever. It would be different this year with him farther away, but I loved his small village and we made plans to be together every two or three weeks.

Back in Lama-Kara I returned to my schoolwork, resigned to the amount of time it took to prepare lessons, correct homework and score tests, with history as an extra subject. Yikes. And when an afternoon became free, I could nourish my appetite for good books, tasty meals and crafts projects. Hmmmm…should I crochet today? Attempt a new sauce? Design some different stationery? Practice the guitar to a rapt audience of compound children? I attempted a tie-dye project, thinking of the bright multi-colored t-shirts that were emblematic of the free speech, anti-war and civil rights campaigns back in the States. I wasn't sure if the resulting creations appeared as accidental as they were, but even I was impressed. And I thought of the twists my life had taken and detected a connection to the irregular zigzag patterns woven into the tie-dyed cloth.

It was finally mango season! I was regionally famous for the sweet orange concoction I produced this time of year. Friends delivered great bundles of softening bright orange mangoes, which I peeled and tossed into a pot with water, cooking gently for an hour or two. I added sugar to the pulpy porridge, then mashed and filtered the mixture, pouring it into jars, cans, bowls. We called it Mango Compôte—much more appealing than Mango Mush, which is what it really was, and I presented gifts of this to the nuns, my friends around town, and especially to my guitar teacher. Chris, another Peace Corps volunteer, and I had a win-win arrangement: he got all the Mango Compôte he wanted and I got guitar lessons. Chris was a small guy for the big sound he made on his 12-string guitar. I'd sit across from him in the middle of my compound awed by his range and technical skills. He could as easily play Rodrigo's "*Concierto de Aranjuez*" as the Beatles' "Let It Be." I loved listening to him and learning a new chord progression each lesson, grimacing as I pushed my fingers to move in positions that didn't seem possible. He was calm and encouraging and didn't wince at my frequent mistakes. I sighed and offered him another jar of compôte. I learned to be careful handling mangoes, remembering a mango marathon Polly, André and I had celebrated recently over one weekend. On a mobylette ride, we stopped to rest in the shade of a leafy manguier and proceeded to pluck as many mangoes as we could, then eagerly accepting the challenge of peeling fresh mangoes with our lips and devouring the sweet juicy flesh.

I awoke the next day with the skin around my mouth swollen and stinging.

"You look like a clown!" Polly exclaimed, pointing to a red rash.

"Mango chapped lips," I diagnosed. The rash became a blister, and stayed for several more days. Mango skin allergy. from then on, I didn't dare let my lips touch mango skin and I always washed my hands after peeling the soft sweet fruit.

I practiced the guitar as often as I could, belting out ballads like "Leaving On A Jet Plane" or running through "*Guantanamera*" with a

Spanish accent. The compound kids froze and stopped their activities when they heard me play, applauding at the end of each song. They thought I was amazing. My fingers moved more and more easily and my small repertoire stretched to entertain me many afternoons. I became less self-conscious and although I'd perfected all three parts of "Rock My Soul", I still didn't come close to being as good as Polly.

In a move of magnanimity, I gifted Edith, the Peace Corps nurse, a jar of compôte. She pooh-poohed our concerns about mango skin allergy. Few others had an allergic reaction like mine. However, she took other household hazards more seriously and tried to caution us. Between house cleaning, cooking, changing seasons, moving about after dark and just living on the edge of the African savannah, there was plenty to avoid. One morning I awakened barely able to see, my eyes swollen shut again, this time from a spider bite. Though the swelling kept me home from school for the day, this rarely happened. Most spiders were swiftly dispatched by lizards. I got used to the lizards and Sundia did her part in relegating the lizard population to high places.

Ah, Sundia! In the middle of one night I was awakened by the plop of my kitty jumping on the bed, skillfully navigating under the mosquito net. I heard a squeak and opened my eyes to see a near-dead mouse on my pillow.

"Aieeee!" I screeched, jumped out of bed and ran out of the bedroom where I looked up and, awake now, saw a bat flying wildly around the living room. *Chauve souris* was their name in French: bald mice. I associated bats with rabies and froze in my light cotton nightgown. Eventually I tiptoed outside into the courtyard, where it was dark and empty, proceeded up the steps to my neighbor's room, tapped on the door, and asked *le monsieur* to come scare the bat out of my house and remove the now dead mouse. He did, readily and in good spirits. Grateful to be a member of his compound family, I thanked him with a jar of compôte.

There were endless flies, beetles, wasps, ants, lightning bugs, worms and crickets. I learned to live with them. As Edith had advised, I took precautions and boasted a well-equipped first aid kit. And to my great regret, I hadn't taken any hikes since arriving in Togo because there was too great a danger of encountering snakes.

Early one morning on my way into school I came upon a circle of excited students huddled around one of the courtyard trees.

"Look *Mees! Regardez! Attention!* Careful where you go!" They directed my view to the tail end of a large snake writhing from a lower branch. Its detached other end—the front half—wiggled in wild circles directly below on the recently swept dirt floor. I gasped and stepped back as the girls grabbed my arms and sidled close to me. I learned that on their way to morning classes, two students had spotted this snake, turning and twisting in the air, its tail wound around the tree branch.

"Aieeeeeee!" they'd screamed hugging each other tightly while Félix, the school's oldest employee and *chef* of maintenance, came running, macheté in hand. With one swift graceful sweep of his arm, he'd sliced the snake in half.

I came upon the scene at that instant and observed both ends of the serpent flail in their final loopy moves. Not a single African I'd met would let a snake live. We didn't learn what kind of snake this was or whether it was dangerous. It was killed straight away. Alarmed, I continued to breathe rapidly long after the snake had been destroyed. What if I'd come upon it alone? Would I have seen it? How many snakes had I already passed? Eventually, we all marched off to morning lessons. I was shaky throughout the day. My students were amused. Unsure whether the visions were real or fueled by my fear, I saw snakes everywhere for the next few days: in coils of rope at the market, in the swirling trails of water along the river and in random curls of branches along the road. I was so afraid of snakes!

Another disturbance, more personal, was revealed one day after school when I was at Chez Herbert, delivering jars of fresh compôte and buying brochettes. Nearly every weekday Herbert grilled delicious goat brochettes over a simple bar-b-q, while his wife, Dada, fried potatoes in a huge metal pan. This was Lama-Kara's popular version of take-out food and everything was usually sold out before I got there. Today I was lucky. Herbert, Dada and their five children were my good friends. We greeted each other cheerfully, and then Dada addressed me unusually tentatively as she wrapped my *brochettes* in newspaper.

"*Mademoiselle,*" she queried, "*tu es toujours avec Monsieur le Policier?*" She asked if I was still dating André.

"*Mais oui!*" I assured her that I was. She nodded, smiled, handed me the sizzling brochettes, and I left. But I wondered about her question. That was awfully personal, I thought. I'd ask André about it when I next saw him. I rode home on my mobylette only semi-conscious of a slight edginess I felt. Had I drunk too many cups of Nescafe earlier? Why this anxiety?

It was easy, a nice morning stroll, though my heart was pounding
and popping...I hopped across the road like a scared cricket and
pushed through a shed...It was just beginning to get light.

—MARIA THOMAS, *African Visas*

EARLY SUNDAY MORNING

IT WAS ANOTHER EARLY SUNDAY MORNING and I was again
feeling so glad to have moved. I loved everything about my new place:
the new collection of joyful kids, the steady supply of water, the nearby
latrine in spite of its mosquitoes and cockroaches, and my new location
on the outskirts of town. Normally I celebrated the luxury of my one
non-teaching day by staying in bed past daybreak listening to the sounds
of women stoking their predawn fires, sticks crackling and dried leaves

Early morning in the Kara Valley

popping. I could hear the children tote water around the compound, asking in sleepy voices where to place the pots and what was next for them to do. Sometimes on Sundays I awoke to the musical chatter of birds competing for ripe mangoes or alerting one another to risks: brooding clouds, a pack of hungry and emaciated dogs, or bigger, noisier birds. But this Sunday morning was different. I was out of bed and on my way before anyone had a chance to notice the change in my routine. I longed for a normal Sunday.

After a brisk and fretful fifteen-minute walk, I reached my destination, and circled the building, passed the main entrance, and entered through a side door. The room was in alarming disarray. Dirtied wads of cloth were scattered about, a few rags clumped together on one long table and others formed an abstract pattern on the floor. They were bloodied, and I stared at the dark red splotches against a background of white chalky walls. I stood silently and attempted to hide my distress. Finally, my friend Michel entered and he, too, was openly disturbed surveying the scene. He turned to greet the approaching doctor.

"*Bonjour.*" Their voices echoed in the empty room as they exchanged handshakes and controlled smiles. I nodded at the doctor who looked official enough. He wore a white coat and moved about the room with confidence. The men spoke briefly in a language I couldn't understand. Michel turned to me and said, "I'll be waiting at this same door. *Du courage.*" He wished me well, and then walked out. I swallowed hard as he left the room. Though I was perspiring, my body felt cold.

This was my first hospital visit in Togo. In spite of an insect bite that closed one eye for two days, monthly bouts of dysentery, a mango skin rash and a nasty stubbed toe, I'd managed to avoid doctors and clinics here. Polly and I had been allowed to work in the distant north because we were strong and healthy. We weren't likely to need the health services readily available in the south, heavily utilized by less hardy volunteers. Anne, my roommate in Lomé with the train case of medicine, had been placed appropriately in the capital city. Polly and I were proud of our healthy bodies and courageous attitudes. After the malaria incident, I'd dedicated myself to listening more carefully to medical advice. I was grateful that Peace Corps had placed me far away. Bolstered by swift recoveries to previous health problems, I still felt invincible.

Until I learned that I was pregnant. Pregnant? I didn't believe it. It was surely the malaria medicine, the heat, the change in my diet, the radical differences in climate from so much traveling. That's why my period is late. That explains it. I'd been vigilant about birth control. In an effort to regain health and strength after my bout with malaria, I'd moved from taking birth control pills to using the diaphragm. Everyone I trusted claimed that the diaphragm was close to 100% effective, I reminded myself.

André and I had had long conversations about the risks a romance carried. We had been very, very careful. Pregnant? Impossible! What could I do? This was terrible bad luck. If anyone found out, beyond André and my closest friends, I'd be sent home. Sent home to the disapproval of my mother and her friends. Sent home ashamed and humiliated. Peace

Corps had strict rules about unmarried pregnant volunteers. There were none. In spite of the campaigning that feminists like Betty Freidan and Gloria Steinem had done to raise awareness of women's rights, these continued to be tough times for women, conservative times. Having a child at 24 was not an option for me and abortions were illegal, expensive, and risky.

What to do? Where to go? I was at the beginning of a blossoming teaching career that was about to crumble. I was desperate. In haste, I dedicated myself to a life of celibacy. But it was too late. What could I do? I loved Togo and my life in Lama-Kara. I was making progress in the three languages I used to negotiate smoothly from south to north, city to village. My efforts at classroom discipline were paying off, and my bargaining techniques at the *marché* were getting bolder and more successful with weekly practice. I didn't want to leave!

I sent an urgent letter via personal courier to Polly an hour south. There was no one else I could talk to. André was away and there was no way to reach him. I scheduled an emergency get-together with Polly for the following weekend. As soon as we met, I revealed my dilemma.

"Oh no!" she said, unsuccessful at hiding her panic, which, of course, increased mine. "Does André know? Does he have any ideas? Can he help?" I explained that André was out of town on a work mission, and I couldn't reach him. Together, Polly and I schemed the safest and most confidential strategy: consult Michel.

"Ask Michel what to do. Or I will. He's in town. I'll get some information."

The next time we talked she spoke with uncharacteristic authority. "Michel can arrange a secret abortion. You'll use a month and a half's salary plus some savings to pay a local doctor. It'll be OK. You'll be OK. Now hurry up and arrange things. I'll come up as soon as I can."

Why me? Why now? What had I done wrong? I'd been so careful! Peace Corps had been very clear about the risks of getting pregnant. Abortions were strictly illegal, but I didn't see any other option. Polly had reassured me I'd be OK. No one would know. I had to trust her. I wanted to trust her. But I was terrified.

As soon as I told him, Michel, one of my first friends and a rejected sweetheart, responded sympathetically.

"Um-hmmm," he said, sizing up the predicament. I was relieved at his lack of judgment. "I'll think about what we can do and keep the matter private." I looked into his eyes, for we were the same height, and said again how thankful I was for his help. He told me to relax, to understand that my predicament was not uncommon, and to trust him.

After several days of intricate arrangements, he met me in this "medical" room strewn with bloodied rags. I began to tremble, nervous and emotional. The doctor detected my terror and finally, nodded a smile. Then he explained the procedure and with one long sweep of his arm, wiped the rags off the table. He assisted me up onto the bench and had me take long, deep breaths. He didn't speak. Why didn't he talk? Was he horrified at what I'd done? Does this confirm the stereotype that all American women are promiscuous? Sinful? How would I ever recover?

There were just the two of us in this cold, empty room. No nurses to smile at me lovingly, no assistants passing tools or towels to the doctor.

No lights, no blankets, no one's hand to squeeze. I had never felt more alone. Confused by a combination of guilt and victimization, I prayed silently for forgiveness and resented my bad luck. I hoped desperately that this silent African professional *médécin* was competent and that this was not the first time he'd performed such a procedure. I prayed that I'd heal swiftly and get on with my life, my work and my vow to avoid men. No more sex.

The doctor suggested that I continue my slow breathing, as there would be no anesthesia. He went straight to work. The nausea I was beginning to feel from fear was suddenly eclipsed by sharp, shooting pains through my groin. I held my breath, exhaled, and prayed, alternating between relinquishing control and accepting responsibility. The doctor worked quickly and it was over in fifteen minutes. It seemed like half a day had passed.

"*Ça va?*" he asked, indicating that it was over. He asked how I was feeling. I didn't know how to answer. French failed me then, lying helpless, frightened and in pain.

"*C'est fini, Mademoiselle. C'est tout. Restez-ici.*" He told me to stay on the table then left the room. I lay there, relieved though sweating heavily and suffering from severe cramps. I went in and out of bouts of shaking, trying to calm myself by exhaling and reminding myself that the worst was over. It didn't feel like the worst was over, but I had to trust what he'd said.

Eventually, fifteen, thirty, maybe sixty minutes passed, and I felt strong enough to sit up. I rose, swiveled slowly so that my legs hung off the edge of the table, willed away more shaking, and tried to avoid glimpsing the bloodied rags on the floor. My face felt hot, my head light. I remembered to breathe deeply, in and out, and attempted to steady myself. Maybe this had been a bad dream. What just happened? Where was I?

Michel reentered the room as I was still struggling to get my balance on the table.

"Michel!" I whispered forcefully. I was happy to see him. "I'm so glad you've come back. Can we leave? Please?!" He urged me to stay longer and rest, but I feigned strength and convinced him to take me home. "*Allons!* Get me out of here!" I pleaded.

We walked out the same side door I'd entered, still early enough on Sunday morning to avoid curious onlookers. He supported me to the car, helped me sit, and drove slowly, going extra gently over bumps and across holes in the dirt road. We finally pulled up to the yellow walls of my compound. He walked me to my front door and into my tiny bedroom where he set me on the bed and put a large jar of boiled, filtered water on the table at my side.

"*Reposes-toi pour quelques jours.* Relax for the next few days," he advised. "Everything will be fine if you give your body time to heal."

"Thank you, Michel," I said, weakly and tearfully. "*Merci pour <u>tout</u>.*" Thank you for <u>everything</u>. You're such a good friend. I will always be grateful for this.

I lay in bed all day, groaning softly, aching and weary from the physical and emotional trauma. I napped briefly, tried to read but couldn't focus, napped again. In the late afternoon, just before sunset, I heard the put-putting of André's Vespa. At first I believed I was dreaming. I didn't expect to see him for several days. Oh gosh. What would I say to him?

He appeared at my bedroom door, announcing he'd returned early from a work assignment and had come for a surprise visit. It was Sunday after all, and he knew I'd be home. Still peeling off his gloves and helmet, he was surprised to see me in bed.

"*Ça va?* Are you sick <u>again</u>? What in the world did you eat last night?"

"*Non, non,*" I told him, half smiling for the first time that day. "I'm not sick. I didn't eat anything strange. It's something else, something more serious. Come closer, come here." He approached me and sat down on the narrow wooden frame of the bed.

"I was pregnant. *J'étais enceinte.*" I began crying, relieved to finally talk about the frightening, lonely ordeal I'd experienced in the early morning. I was so relieved to have him here.

Stunned, his eyes got wide and his silence made me nervous, afraid, sweaty. Then he finally spoke. "Tell me," he said. "I'm here with you now. Tell me everything."

I spoke slowly as my eyes filled with tears. André hovered, removing his shirt and placing it neatly on the floor, not taking his eyes off me. Then he removed his pants with one hand continuing to cling to my arm with the other. He hung his pants on the door of my armoire. In his t-shirt and shorts, he lifted the cotton cover and crawled onto the bed beside me. Letting go of my hand, he wrapped his arms around me gently, and we rocked back and forth as I told my story.

Peace of mind is proportional to giving up control; things happen when they happen, or don't often for no discernible reason. The best strategy is usually to trust that things will work out. Sometimes they do.

—**JULIAN SMITH**, *Crossing the Heart of Africa: An Odyssey of Love and Adventure*

RESTLESS

MY PHYSICAL RECOVERY WAS SWIFT, but the emotional fallout lingered. Guilt, lost confidence, less lightheartedness stayed with me. The secrecy of it all helped me pretend it had never happened. And my teaching schedule swept me back into busy-ness; it didn't allow for interruptions. Each day began thirty minutes after sunrise when my neighbor's radio blasted the 6:30 musical alarm. At 8:00 I rushed to school.

On the road out of Lama-Kara

Classes proceeded nonstop, one after the other until noon. I had to be on my toes with my students, "on" every second. Feeling sad or sick or tired didn't excuse anyone. "*Ça ne va pas!*" Sister Kathérine's reprimand rang in my ears when the slightest irregularity surfaced for anyone. I was feeling guilty for lots of things.

After morning classes there was a three-hour break that gave everyone a chance to head home for lunch and take a short nap, though I rarely was able to sleep. And besides, in spite of the heat, the morning's pace made it impossible for me to relax. Even if I had been able to manage a siesta, there were afternoon tasks yet to tackle: gather materials for art class, get a head start on dinner prep, catch up on corrections. We returned to work from 3-5, when I taught two more classes. Finally, back home at the end of the work day, there was the rush to prepare for the next day's English lessons before sundown at 6. Six AM to six PM. Twelve hours of light every day year round made for short days, but refreshingly predictable. Still, the daily push for staying abreast of teaching and living felt relentless.

"I've never done anything so challenging," I wrote home well into my second year of teaching. Lots about my life in Togo was challenging, but I singled out my work as I tried to give friends and family a hint of what my teaching involved. Even with a year's experience behind me and a range of techniques to keep my students attentive, lesson prep and corrections were so utterly demanding that I had little time for anything else.

Sister Kathérine had explained that tight monitoring kept Collège Adèle girls on task and in line, "*disciplinées*" she called it, so we were required to give tests and a course grade every four weeks. This exam schedule, on top of daily lesson plans, weekly quizzes and comprehensive finals, made for a monumental workload. My responsibilities were compounded because of my many courses: four levels of English, Art, P.E. and my new bonus class, West African history. I taught more classes than any of the nuns, I whined to myself. Then I took heart. They had such faith in my teaching! I was gaining great experience! But as the school year wore on and I was inundated with papers to correct, quizzes to design, grammar points to review and lessons to plan, I suspected that it was my willingness more than my ability that had me prepping, teaching and testing seven classes. Oh, those wily nuns. That scheming Soeur Directrice!

I was finally healthy, recovered from a string of minor medical mishaps, and determined to steer clear of any more ailments. Now I understood why my Edith's Inn roommate Anne had come to Togo with her silly suitcase full of medicine. I continued to resist "medicaments" beyond my anti-malaria pills when I could and resolved repeatedly to be careful. *Prevenir c'est mieux que guerir.* "It's better to prevent than to cure" was added to my collection of proverbs. I wasn't alone in having experienced medical mishaps. Polly had recently been evacuated with a rare form of meningitis. She'd returned now, and was recovering, but for two strong young women, we'd each exhibited some vulnerability.

One Friday I walked into class, having run out of time to prepare, exhausted at week's end and decided on the spot to present a lesson on current events.

"Today I'm going to talk about The Women's Liberation Movement." I described the campaign for equal rights that had captured the imagination and activism of many, at least in my northern California community, and I ended up filling the whole class period presenting what my students thought were odd trends and radical ideas. I spoke as if I'd planned the lesson. I was ready to open the minds of these Collège Adèle girls.

"In America," I announced, making sweeping general statements, "men, not just women, do the cooking; women, not just men, get paid for driving buses, building houses, and gardening. Women drive trucks!" I continued, telling them about Zero Population Growth and birth control and women who chose to divorce. My students laughed. They couldn't believe what I'd told them. One girl raised her hand and asked, "Do men hit their wives where you live?"

"If they do, the police come and arrest them," I replied. The girls applauded, convinced that life in America was both entertaining and kind to women. But it didn't seem real to them. I was tempted to stir these girls up again, to continue my "women's rights" lectures and talk more openly. I found them exhausted and repressed by the work they were expected to do, trapped in the roles dictated by their history and traditions. Although these women were beautiful, smart, luckier than most, their roles as women were so limited. I wondered what their attitudes were. Did they think their roles were fair? What did their brothers, fathers, uncles believe? In spite of these musings, I stopped at this Friday and resisted returning to politically hot topics. Peace Corps would approve of my restraint. As guests in countries around the world, volunteers had been continually advised not to discuss political topics. It was inappropriate and naïve. So I reverted to singing on Fridays when I hadn't had time to plan. "I'm a Little Teapot" stepped in for Women's Liberation. Friday's presentation may not have had an effect on my students, but it reminded me that my complaints about being overworked were pretty trivial when compared to the burdens these girls had to bear.

Mercifully, the government scheduled many holidays, some calendared long in advance and others announced at the last minute. On these days off, I joined friends on mobylette rides to outlying villages or headed south to visit André. If it happened to be market day in Kétao, I was eager to buy some white cotton fabric we called Kabré cloth, woven only in the north by local women, and available only at this market. The large fringed pieces softened with each wash and were unique and attractive. I used mine as tablecloth, bedspread, and picnic blanket. When in Kétao, I also visited Jim, another Peace Corps volunteer, who, unaccustomed to living without a washing machine, did his laundry by dipping clothes into a basin of water then hanging them up to dry. No soap, no scrubbing, no wringing. Amused by his method, I asked if his jeans stayed as stiff as they looked on the line. I suggested that he hire help or use soap, but he ignored me. How far I'd come in my attitude about giving local people opportunities to work.

On the bumpy dirt paths in and out of villages on excursions, we passed kids and men on bicycles precariously hauling goats, pots, wood, bags of flour and crates of ignams. I looked for crafts like the name stamp or the balançoir, continually increasing my growing collection of useful and attractive souvenirs.

I loved heading south and visiting Bafilo not only because I got to spend time with André, but because the village was small and green and beautiful; the people were friendly and life was slow and simple. As usual, I wanted to see André more than he was available. His schedule was unpredictable and I was frustrated with what seemed like long periods of waiting between visits. I began spending more time with other friends but I was so happy when André and I were able to coordinate a reunion.

He greeted me with my favorite invitation to a hug.

"Dans mes bras! Dans mes bras!" and I fell into his arms as if it'd been a year instead of a few weeks.

It was unexpectedly fun being a policier's girlfriend. Nearly all the policemen in the region recognized me and waved when they saw me pass. More than once they'd warned me about a blocked road if President Eyadema was visiting his natal village in the north or alerted me to a rockslide or series of huge puddles, and rainy day disasters. My movie star status, in relation to André's role as a policier at least, had finally become tolerable. This marked a new and different way of facing onlookers. During weekends in Andre's village, I caught up on schoolwork, read, knit, or if I was lucky, watched the birth of a lamb or the hatching of chicks. Together, we listened to music on the radio—Highlife, Afrobeat, Soukous—dancing all by ourselves in his small house and eating sauces brimming with fresh okra, spinach and tomatoes.

Recently our relationship had become slightly strained, or at least I felt distance growing between us. I attributed the discomfort to my summer traveling, medical mishaps and to his new post. My concern about us was fueled by the continuing questions from acquaintances in Lama-Kara. On this visit I asked him why people kept asking me if we were still together. Why all the questions?

"Pourquoi toujours des questions de nous deux?" Why were people so curious? I assumed they were nosey, digging into our personal lives and hungry for gossip. It was part of the restlessness of living where not much happened, I figured. My coming and going over the last months was ripe

material for speculation. André responded readily but I wasn't prepared for what he said.

"*Les gens parlent? Ah ha.*" Long pause. "*J'ai quelques nouvelles je dois te dire.*" Another pause. "*J'étais avec une autre pendant ton absence.*" Punctuated by pauses, he told me he had news. He'd taken up with another girl while I'd been on vacation in Europe.

"*Pardon?!*" I wasn't sure I'd understood. He repeated, slowly, that he hadn't been *fidèl,* loyal, when I'd been away over the summer.

I felt sick to my stomach. My eyes filled with tears and my body turned cold. I trembled with a mixture of embarrassment, anger, betrayal, and shame. No wonder everyone kept asking. They must have seen André with her. I didn't know what to say, what to think. André reached for my hand. I recoiled.

"*Mais on ne se voit plus.*" André said he wasn't seeing her any longer. I remained silent and slightly numb while the dream of a future together flashed and crashed.

"*C'est fini. Elle ne m'interesse plus,*" he continued. "*C'est toi, ma Bubu, mon amour.*" André attempted to reassure me that I was his girl and that it had been only a brief escapade. While this gave me fleeting comfort, I wasn't sure what to think, how to feel. Could I ever trust him again? What about my plans for our future? What about all that's happened in the past?

As stunned and horrified as I was, I thought about my behavior during our time apart and my flirtations with Rudy and my male nurse friends at the Frankfurt hospital. I realized that I could easily have taken up with one of them. I hadn't, but I hadn't been entirely innocent either. It's not like a fling hadn't occurred to me. I cried, I took heart, I shivered.

We spent the rest of the afternoon working our way past André's affair through tears, music, cooking, and lovemaking. I allowed my need for emotional reassurance to overcome my doubt. Whatever would I do without André in my life? I couldn't imagine a better boyfriend or living in this place without the security and affection he offered. I wanted to be André's sweetheart and I wanted him to choose me. So I saw this as a new beginning. It was an opportunity to strengthen our love. It didn't take long to convince myself of his sincerity. We pledged absolute loyalty to one another. I forgave André; he affirmed his love for me. Our future together was reestablished.

I returned to Lama-Kara from an emotional weekend in the village drained but relieved, and no choice but to jump back into a busy schedule. While the days followed one another somewhat predictably, the nights were full of surprises. And the nighttime activity was not on the streets or in the clubs—it was in my head. Likely induced by malaria preventative medicine, I had a seething dream life. One morning I woke up after having shown my father around Lomé. In another dream I was spending time with my childhood dog and suddenly lost my vision. I bolted up in my bed, forcing my eyes open. I groaned with anxiety and relief at having lost then regained my ability to see. In another, I panicked that my high school boyfriend was pursuing me still, having tracked me down in Togo. I breathed restlessly until I realized it had been a dream. What drama! Other dreams reflected my current restlessness, the weight of decisions ahead as they ushered me in and out of malarial hallucinations, or replayed an obstinate student's refusal to do what I'd instructed in the classroom. One out of every six scary, ominous, alarming dreams was balanced by a comforting sensation of being back home with people I loved doing something pleasant. In one, I was sitting at home on a weekend afternoon with my mom and sister in the sunny back yard or watching Perry Como on TV Sunday night. The frightening dreams mystified me because I was feeling so well-adjusted, *si bien habituée*.

Indeed, life had attained a certain stability, and because I now lived in a comfortable compound, my teaching routine became increasingly manageable. I had friends not far away and most letters from home eventually hiccupped their way to me. But I began to worry about Life After Peace Corps. And worry I did. Questions bubbled up around me. Should I extend and stay a third year in Togo? Should I start job searching at home? Should I look for a different job in Africa? The U.S. economy

Countryside around Lama-Kara

was terrible—would I find work in the States? What jobs were available? Could I qualify? I privately considered marrying André as often as I thought about leaving him in Togo and moving on. A cross-cultural marriage would never work. My parents hadn't make good on their promise to visit me, so a family reunion could have to be the result of my doing the traveling. One day I decided to return home. The next day I decided to stay a third year.

I got to know most corners of Lama-Kara and the northern region, becoming increasingly restless. I headed south to Lomé more often, surrendering willingly to the six-to-seven-hour journey by "bush taxi."

Lomé now, on my terms, offered a new frontier. I took advantage of tennis lessons, fresh fruit and European restaurants—a sharp contrast to what was available in Lama-Kara and what I'd been interested in when I'd first arrived. I tried not to spend most of my monthly allowance in one visit. I stayed with friends in fancy new Peace Corps housing and made peace with Edith who seemed contrite after her malaria misdiagnosis. Polly and I met waves of new volunteers. I escaped the harmattan, the cold, dry wind that blew dust off the Sahara. The humid weather of the south was a relief from the grit of desert sand.

I got better acquainted with different neighborhoods in Lomé and could enjoy an afternoon at the beach, aware of where it was safe, clean and pleasant to sunbathe. I would move away from what looked like the carcass of a dog, girls fetching water or a crab crazily crisscrossing the tide where the undertow left a steep drop along the shore. If I stayed late enough at the beach, meeting friends and going for a drink at a brasserie nearby, I'd look up at the starry sky over the tops of gently swaying palm trees, and see nearly as many stars as I had spotted in the north. The air was soft and warm. I spent time with ex-patriots, easier now that I understood and spoke faster French. What a switch from the early days when I hadn't wanted to be seen with a European, when I hated Lomé, and when I couldn't wait to return to Lama-Kara. What was happening to me?

"I miss peaches, American music, chocolate chip cookies and washing machines," I whined to my mother in a cassette tape I sent home. No longer was I rolling out ten letters on a weekend, each personalized with my name stamp, a hand-stenciled design, a doodle. I was more involved in my life in Togo, spending less time alone, so correspondence with folks at home was more sporadic. Cassette tapes had made communication more immediate and direct. I was able to record my students' singing, my neighbor's greetings and my slowly advancing guitar playing. I sent home recordings of Bella Bellow, Togo's beloved young female vocalist. In exchange, I received a recording of Arthur Fiedler conducting the Boston Pops and my mother's exuberant account of another pet adoption. My dad and stepmom sent news of their busy social life.

"Hello Daughter," my father began. "Mary Beth! Mary Beth!" my stepmom chimed in, customizing my name and describing a recent home improvement or travel adventure. Hearing everyone's voice from far away and long ago made me homesick. The mail still took 2-4 weeks to arrive, but the tapes served to reduce the time and distance between us.

There was so much of my life in Togo that I now took for granted. I never used my left hand to greet another or hand off an item. (The left hand was reserved for unpleasant tasks.) I used my red pen for correcting student papers ONLY. (If you wrote letters with red ink, it meant someone had died.) I didn't sing in the shower (bad luck), didn't ask any visitors if they were hungry (everyone was always hungry), and I made sure to extend the regional greeting to everyone before saying anything else. It was insulting not to greet them first. Every night I drank *citronelle* tea by boiling blades of grass that grew so plentifully outside the compound. I continued to pay an older man, my *blanchisseur*, not quite 40 cents every week to collect, wash, iron and return clean clothes. André and I wore outfits of matching fabric, publicly showcasing our solidarity; my small flower garden continued to offer yellow, coral, and fuchsia zinnia blossoms, and I delighted in taking showers in my sunny stall next to the bananier. I could stay here forever. Should I?

The compound kids still cheered at the two-cent beignets I continued to buy for them each week. I also continued dropping off treats on visits to my former neighbors in the compound in the center of town. I stopped by on market days, and wondered how I ever survived living for a year in this busy noisy hub. Mama Twins had a new baby on her back, the older twins already toddling, and Oncle Claude's nephews had moved into my space. There was talk of paving the main street of town and remodeling the military hotel. Life and Lama-Kara were moving ahead. I was ready to move ahead too. Should I jump aboard, embrace this life forever and settle down, or should I jump ship and move on?

PARADE

FOUR TRIUMPHANT STUDENTS ran toward me on the dirt road in the bright sun of an African midmorning. Jostling themselves into formation, they were a ragtag band of jubilant female marchers leading a procession, colorful drapes of African cloth flying off their shoulders as they shouted, laughed and gulped for air between happy cries. They kicked up dust scampering forward to meet me as the heat pressed into our skin and we hastened to the shade of a mango tree. Here we paused,

Students testing their pinwheels

on a field trip near the end of the school year, the first away-from-the-school experience for these students and the first for me in Togo. The girls were going to try out our hand-crafted paper pinwheels as we made our way to a picnic spot, some running, others trying to run in tight skirts, and the rest walking behind, balancing baskets of food, drinks and games. All was color, movement, joy.

"*Tiens-là plus haut!*" Élizabeth called to Dabiétou, telling her to thrust her pinwheel higher to catch a breeze.

"*Plus vite! Beaucoup plus vite!*" Cathérine told her to run faster.

"*Mees!! Mees! Peetchuh! Peetchuh!*" Asupui called to me, commanding a photo in her version of *Franglais* which I had no trouble understanding. I adjusted the lens, dialing my Pentax until the girls came into sharp focus and quickly clicked two, three times before they overtook me, all of us nearly collapsing in laughter. So far, no pinwheels had turned. Was it the tight skirts that limited momentum, the lack of a breeze, or perhaps poor pinwheel engineering? Nothing diminished our delight at being outside the white walls of the classroom and away from the restrictions of those intimidating nuns. We were together having fun and feeling free.

We gathered in our shady spot, spread a few faded pagnes over bumpy ground and tiptoed as delicately as we could onto the cloth, all twenty-plus of us finding a place to settle. I watched as the girls helped each other lower their heavy baskets with so much grace and so little apparent effort. I noticed for the hundredth time how my students' work was so physically taxing, but because they always worked together, it was synchronized, making even the toughest jobs look easy. No matter if they were pounding fufu in a polyrhythmic thump-thump-thump-thump of regular beats, or elegantly managing the lifting and unloading of inconceivably long firewood bundles, or collectively planting and harvesting ignams to the music of gentle singing, these traditional female tasks were always elegantly executed. I placed my bag of papers and pens and extra pinwheels in the center of our picnic cloth and swiveled to a seated position, wondering if I'd be able to hold this group together. Would I be able to "control" these rowdy joyous students when neither my language nor my experience gave me much confidence? It had taken weeks to get approval for this adventure. Was I in over my head? How would the girls respond to being outside the classroom? How would they react to such unfamiliar freedom? I hoped desperately that the girls would stay together, have fun, and not challenge my timid authority.

Three girls ran over to me and asked for pinwheels, boasting to the others that they'd be able to make theirs turn. The pinwheels were the product of a combination art and English lesson on following directions using new vocabulary. Students' success at listening carefully and being precise with corners and folds was about to be tested.

"*Comme ça!*" Marielle demonstrated, sweeping the crude toy in an arc over her head as the pinwheel wiggled and began to turn. There were screams and cheers as three more students rose and ran toward me asking for pinwheels so that they too could have a try.

Of my teaching load, four levels of English, history, P.E. and Art, I was most enthusiastic about the art class. It pushed me to be even more resourceful than I'd already learned to be and encouraged me to dream up fabulous projects. Twig patterns! Leaf stencils! Designs inspired from the colorful cloth students wore everyday! Ideas revolved around nearby materials and what I could ask friends to send. With popsicle sticks, glue, index cards, tracing paper, iridescent markers and a stash of colored pencils and paper at school, we'd managed to produce an impressive array of artifacts that were pleasing in process if not particularly functional. Students had proposed the first project—a collection of decorative stationery. Wistful village scenes, embellished proverbs and portraits of women in stunning traditional outfits demonstrated the promise of these young artists. We created stencil prints of leaves using pieces of screen and brushing paint over them with toothbrushes. We rubbed crayons over African mask designs cut from cardboard and layered and glued one over another. We made collages from my old calendar pictures. The pinwheel idea, cutting, curling and fastening a paper square to a long straw, was our most recent project. They were designed to be decorative and functional. Could we actually get them to spin??

"*Aiiieee! Ça marche!* Ees workeeng, Mees!" Élise called as her pinwheel made several successful revolutions. Though they had pledged to speak English throughout the field trip, they were too excited to hold to their agreement and I didn't want to be the Language Police all day, so I reminded them every now and then to at least try to speak English.

"I don't understand you two—what did you say?! Say it in English! Remember that we told Soeur Kathérine this would be English class. She wouldn't have given us permission to leave school if she'd known you'd speak French!" I was deluding myself if I believed anyone would heed my warning. I really sounded like one of the nuns.

When the girls tired of trying to get the pinwheels to turn—we had a modest success rate—with four of the twenty twirling freely, we settled into lunch and enjoyed handfuls of roasted peanuts, peeled mangoes, chicken brochettes and squares of my homemade applesauce cake. Some girls sat in a line, facing the same directions, and braided or rebraided a classmate's hair in fresh geometric patterns or symmetrical loops. Others

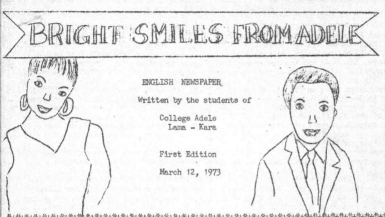

BRIGHT SMILES FROM ADELE

ENGLISH NEWSPAPER

Written by the students of

College Adele
Lama - Kara

First Edition

March 12, 1973

ADELE'S SPORTS TEAM WAKES UP!!!

"It's time!! It's time! Let's go to sports!" We must run to the sports field, but certain girls walk lazily. The others who like sports very much run and do the round of the infirmary and arrive tired on the field. We do some exercises and then when we are ready, everyone runs to the volleyball field. Soon the field is filled with girls. The girls who don't know how to play volleyball are sent out: "Go out! Go out!" We quarrel sometimes. The girls who don't like the noise go out. We begin to play. When the ball goes out, the girls say: "It's your mistake! You let the ball fall!" Sometimes the girl is angry and she walks away. We continue the game. When somebody plays well she laughs, dances or says "It's in my blood!" She boasts. When it's time, we return to class yelling.

One day, when our teacher Miss Pike asked us if we wanted to participate in OSSUT, we made a volleyball team. Some weeks after, we were invited by the lycee girls to play a match. First we were afraid and frightened. Everybody wanted to see this game. The big day, Wednesday arrived. Certain reasons prevented the college from accompanying the players to the lycee. We were lonely and afraid of the crowd. As it was our first match, we were very timid. Our legs were like cotton. The net scared us. Their first serves scared us. They thought that they were better than us. They changed their team and brought the "cadettes". When the cadettes came on the field they made a lot of noise. You should have seen! We be-

lieved that they were excellent players. One girl on our team served; she made 7 points. That showed us they weren't worth anything. We won. The big girls came back eventually and they beat us. After this match we knew that we needed training and decided to do better. We had a week for that and one Saturday you should have seen! There was technique. We aren't boasting but to be true we made sensible progress. In one word: "We are qualified to play at Lome!" We thank the men who helped us. Now they can say "there are 3 colleges in Lama-Kara!"   ADOYI Mariama, TELOU Euphrasie, AMEGNINOU Elise, KOUSSOUTEMA M.

WHY THE MOON HAS A PICTURE OF A WOMAN

On Sunday a woman went to the farm. God had refused to work on Sunday. God was angry and for the punishment, he took the woman and he threw her in the moon. It's why today we see a picture of the woman in the moon.   PAGNAH Angele

OUR ENGLISH NEWSPAPER

One day in the morning, Miss Pike, our English teacher said to us that we are going to begin an English Newspaper. We are proud to do it and we present it to you for the first time. You will be pleased with our newspaper. This newspaper will speak to you about our thinking. You will be glad after reading this. ABIYI Marcelline, PALI Mathilde, AMONA Veronique, TCHASSI Francoise

Our English newspaper

pulled out the first edition of our English newspaper and took turns reading aloud articles they and other students had written, laughing about spelling mistakes or their Franglais pronunciation.

I was so proud of this newspaper, having doubted that it would ever come to be. It had taken the students weeks to decide what they wanted to include, to write the articles, then finalize corrections. But finally, here it was, an eclectic mix of topics and genres, for us to enjoy on our first field trip."BRIGHT SMILES FROM ADELE, English Newspaper written by the students of Collège Adèle, Lama-Kara, First Edition." There was an account of the school's first volleyball game peppered heavily with English sports vocabulary, demonstrating one advantage an English teacher had filling in as P.E. teacher. Next to this article was a short description of the feast day of Ramadan in Adama's village. In another feature article, six students had interviewed Sister Lorenca and shared an article on the nun who "…disciplines but doesn't lose heart with us, because she loves us like her children." There were riddles, a story about the Fetish Forest where sterile women went to become fertile, an illustration of a Collège Adèle student beside a suited gentleman, and a tale explaining that spiders were small because one once angered an elephant who stomped it down to size. "Why the Moon Has a Picture of a Woman" recounted the story of a woman who went to the farm on a Sunday, defying God's call to rest, and got tossed toward the moon. "The Passage of the Elephant" reported the heroism of the president who had killed an elephant further north and was proudly parading its body on a huge truck south through each major town of the country. An accompanying illustration showed stick figures jumping and dancing as the beast passed. The stories provided an insight into long held cultural beliefs and practices.

The school newspaper was two pages long, excruciatingly typed single-spaced, by me of course. Each quarter-inch of white space had been filled by a potential professional newspaper journalist or illustrator. The result was no white space at all. So we were celebrating this grand accomplishment, its audience precisely the same as its authors. In the warm shade of our afternoon together, students who were not braiding sat in small clusters and practiced reading English, laughing at what I hoped they'd keep and share forever.

When the snacking, reading and hair-braiding wound down, some girls returned to their pinwheels and vowed to redesign the model. A few of us started a round of volleyball, but it was too hot for exertion so we returned to our shady picnic spot, nibbled more food and chatted. I was

Relaxing on our field trip

not part of most conversations, but I smiled and looked around at the girls, reassuring myself that the awkwardness I felt was normal. As hard as I'd tried to live like a local, I wasn't a local, and this truth, finally, was becoming acceptable to me. Everyone else, of course, had known this all along. Even so, my students and I had never ever been so close together in such a relaxed setting. I thought about the freedom of being outside the classroom, away from the school. I wondered if the students were feeling the same intimacy I was feeling. I had brief, polite conversations with Elise, Berthe and Elizabeth, but for most of the afternoon I sat and watched while the girls chatted and giggled.

When the sun signaled the end of the school day, we slowly, reluctantly, started to pack our baskets. We folded the pagnes, surveyed our picnic spot feeling sad that the adventure was coming to a close, and unhurriedly began the walk back to school. Many students dawdled arm-in-arm, some draped themselves over their classmates' shoulders in spite of the bulky loads they carried. Marçelline began singing. "So high, can't get over it, so low, can't get under it..." and a few others joined her, adding gestures we had practiced in class while memorizing this verse of our favorite song. Soon everyone was singing, all three parts to "Rock My Soul", the activity we'd reserved for Fridays as a reward if students had turned in homework and been attentive. This day was its own reward. Like a band of colorful troubadours on a summertime serenade, we entered the school courtyard, singing, clapping and drumming on gourds and plastic basins. Students who'd stayed behind at school stopped what they were doing as we arrived and watched, stunned. The nuns froze in mid-scurry, staring.

The afternoon sun sent light sideways and projected our elongated shadows onto the clean-swept grounds of the school. It was clear to all that something magical had occurred on our day away. We walked in, our happy parade, so jubilant and united, high-stepping and intertwined. I held my breath during this moment, vowing never to forget the enchantment of this day, of our time together.

After the field trip everything about teaching changed. Students never again balked in class. They helped each other read difficult chapters, pitched in when one was facing family troubles at home and flooded me with questions when I rewarded them with news of current events or new 70's protest songs. When we finished a unit, did well on a quiz, got high scores at term's end, we sang, adding "Blowin' in the Wind" and "We Shall Overcome" to our repertoire. Together we explored African history and English at deeper levels. Our art projects became more collaborative and creative, and we even organized a sports day, inviting students from a school farther north to visit and compete for awards in high jump and volleyball.

I began to notice how the girls' drawings developed without any direct instruction on my part. Initially, illustrations had shown students in formal poses, serious figures standing straight beside small earthen homes or single palm trees. Then, some time later, the pictures presented girls in small groups leaning against each other, tressing hair, holding hands or carrying baskets. More recently now, the art had become more complicated and dynamic as it started to include drawings of young women dancing, singing, and smiling. Some of the illustrations even showed the girls returning jubilant from our field trip parade.

"*Mees!! Mees!!* Look*!*" they thrust their pictures at me for approval. "Look *Mees*—we're all together*!!*"

John, our fearless driver, piles the field staff, Tom, and me into the flatbed truck, belongings tightly secured under a tarp in the back. We roar away on a dusty road full of potholes... John solemnly announces the name of each village as we approach, and then plants his hand firmly on the horn as we careen through crowds of men and women carrying bundles of sticks on their heads. People scramble to get out of the way. Children stare, chickens scatter, and we leave a cloud of dust in our wake.

—**MIMI ROBINSON**, *Still It Makes Me Laugh: Impressions of West Africa*

SISTER KATHÉRINE

SISTER KATHÉRINE, la Soeur Directrice, the self-appointed French *guardienne* of Collège Sainte Adèle, continued to torment colleagues, students, staff and community members. All of us, nuns included, walked in fear of her sudden appearance, her beadlike glare, and her harsh commands. She reigned in her empire, the tassled rope belt around her waist swinging wildly, imperiously, as she strutted about the school grounds. Shrieking at students who were late or ill or absent, she

One of many large trucks that broke down en route from Lama-Kara to Lomé

gave a disgusted fling of her habited head, dismissing them with a cluck and a sneer as the most recently humiliated girl walked away in shame.

Sister Kathérine seemed to enjoy the power she wielded. One morning while I was in class, shortly after I'd launched my youngest students on a review of the previous day's lesson, she appeared in my classroom. Silent, though formidable, she stood in front of six rows of wooden desks, each desk occupied by two, or sometimes three, bubbly fifteen-year-old Togolese girls. The chorus of thirty-six singsong voices practicing questions came to an abrupt hush. Before I could welcome her with the requisite *"Bonjour, ma Soeur!"* Sister Kathérine scanned the sea of startled faces, her birdlike glare landing on a student in the back row, one who had been absent for the previous four days.

"Angéline! Viens ici!" Upon Sister Kathérine's command, Angéline shuddered, cowered, bowed her head, and pulled her reluctant body up and out of the creaking wooden desk. She walked slowly toward the front of the room while her classmates echoed her reaction and seemed to shrink around her in solidarity. Two feet from Sister Kathérine, she stopped, head still bowed.

"Angéline! Show your classmates what you have done!" la Soeur spit her words, at once whipping out a piece of paper with her right hand and a cow-tail whip with her left.

"REGARDEZ!!" la Soeur shrieked as she waved the paper overhead for all to see. Then she pummeled Angéline with questions and commands:

"Is this your French literature assignment?'

"Oui, ma Soeur," Angéline responded in nearly a whisper.

"What KIND of student are you, Angéline? Don't you remember it is a PRIVILEGE to attend this school?" Brandishing the papers, she asked,

"Did you submit this homework assignment one week late?"

"*Oui, ma Soeur.*"

"Stand up straight! Look at me! Be respectful! Be respectable!" Angéline raised her head.

"WHY was this late?" Angéline could not explain, of course, that her uncle had fallen ill and that she'd spent the last four days applying wet rags to his fever-ridden forehead, running to adjacent villages to summon the healer, sending a young brother to bring the pharmacist, and preparing a new, stronger broth each day. She couldn't tell the Directrice what she had told me because Collège Adèle students were expected to put their studies first, before family responsibilities. So she remained silent while the nun reached between the papers to pull out another student's assignment, the one Angéline had copied. Sister Kathérine, livid at this act of dishonor, breaking one rule in order not to break another, continued her tirade.

"Collège Sainte Adèle students submit their homework on time! Students at our school are not absent! Students at our school stand up straight! They speak UP!" She finally paused, reduced her voice to a hiss and said, "You are despicable, Angéline," stretching the second syllable so that it sounded evil. Her scowl darkened as she spit out the insult. I wanted to run to Angéline, envelope her in a tight embrace and hasten her away, out of Sister Kathérine's range, away from the dangers of school and her no-win role as a young woman.

Then the nun nodded, Angéline's cue to stand tall, arms outstretched, palms down. Thereupon Sister Kathérine shifted speeds, as if moving suddenly into a higher gear, and began furiously swatting the top of Angéline's small brown hands with the cow-tail, first the right, then the left.

Long wiry strands of hair from the cow-tail flew into the air, with each strike emitting dust and a dirty, musty odor. Angéline flinched each time the cowtail thrashed her, but she did not cry out, withdraw her hands or shift her posture. After six stinging blows, Sister Katherine locked Angéline's eyes in her glare and announced:

"This will NEVER happen again, will it, Angéline?"

"Non, ma Soeur."

"Go back to your seat." The nun turned abruptly, panning the classroom with her ominous scowl, puffed up her shoulders, and walked out of the room.

I felt tiny, shaken, impotent. The students remained silent. After this horrifying incident, I wondered if they'd ever mutiny. Would they rise up and cry out that the responsibilities of home, gathering firewood before dawn, doing all the shopping and cooking for uncles and small brothers and sisters, caring for a dying grandmother, digging in the fields during planting season or walking ten miles to assist a sister with her newborn were just too much on top of school obligations. Did their roles at home make it impossible to complete copying the three pages of sentences from a French grammar lesson, to memorize lines from a Baudelaire poem, or to read dense paragraphs about the Middle Ages? There was something maliciously incongruent for a young African woman who attended a Catholic school. Maybe this applied to any woman in any school. Women who wanted to be educated were doomed in northern Togo. I participated in the push to get these young women to take their studies seriously, but their additional responsibilities constantly sabotaged their success. How did they persevere? How did they survive? Didn't Sister Katherine understand the challenges? Why was she so cruel?

I reasoned that the nuns must have felt as if they'd made great sacrifices too, and I searched for explanations to understand their harsh and unreasonable discipline. They were far from their homes and that must have worn them down. They weren't enjoying the comforts and conveniences of what was familiar to them, after all. Yes, they were making sacrifices, but isn't that what they'd chosen? Living in the north of the country, they depended on regular, although infrequent, supply runs to the south in order to stock up on items they couldn't get in the savannah. They traveled to buy fresh fruits and vegetables, bottled drinks and French cheese, only available in the south. The nuns rarely went on these forays, since it was at least a three or four day trip over washboard roads, subject to unpredictable delays. But on one of these supply runs, Sister Kathérine went along, presiding in the back seat of the school's white Peugeot sedan, bouncing to the vibrations of the car as it sped south, dodging lines of women on the road carrying baskets of cloth, firewood, pots of water from the river, swerving around emaciated cows or coming upon overcrowded trucks, speeding recklessly and listing dangerously to one side or the other.

For this trip, the sisters had handed over a longer than normal shopping list. So while Sister Kathérine did errands in the capital city, Félix, Collège Adèle's all around maintenance fellow, stocked up on boxes of sugar, cartons of French wine, bags of flour, rice, and a several-month supply of bottled drinks: carbonated water, sodas, juice. He packed the Peugeot with attention to every two-inch space available. By the time the errands were completed and the shopping done, Sister Kathérine was resettled in the back seat, tucked between shoulder-high boxes on each side and in front of several rows of bottles on the ledge at her back. The packed vehicle took off early in the morning, traveling more slowly than usual, the extra weight challenging the Peugeot's power. They planned to be back in Lama-Kara in two days.

The first part of the trip north went smoothly. The main road running north from the capital city was paved for the first 300 kilometers. It was narrow, barely accommodating two large vehicles, but it was paved, so if cars stuck to the proper side of the road, the first part of the south-to-north trip was usually swift and relatively comfortable. At the midway mark, the tarmac became dirt, and the second half of the drive was torturous. The washboard stretches became deep gullies in many spots. In other places, and especially after a rainstorm, the road disappeared altogether. Northern Togo didn't boast tall mountains, but it did have a few hills, and the road wound around and between these hills. It could be treacherous if you happened upon other vehicles, or villagers, or animals.

So as the packed Peugeot ventured north, tilting more than usual at bends and recovering speed on the straight sections, it made decent time, driver and passenger envisioning an early arrival. But at one of the numerous curves, not distinctive in any way until this day, the Peugeot met another vehicle, an enormous empty truck careening into the other side of the road at high speed. The collision was sudden and nearly silent as the truck's grill swallowed the front end of the Peugeot and muffled the sounds of metal, rubber and glass as everything was smashed, crashed and broken.

It took nearly thirty minutes for the truck driver to pull himself through the broken window of the crumpled cabin door and climb down to see the devastation. By then, villagers had appeared and were running frantically about the car, unable to rescue the trapped passengers. Miraculously, Félix survived, the grill of the oncoming truck having protected his body like a metal airbag. Sister Kathérine was less fortunate. Upon impact, the bottles behind her head flew in every direction, exploding into hundreds of pieces of miniature multi-edged razor-sharp knives. Like tiny glass daggers, they slashed through the car's upholstery and boxes of supplies, cracking the windows, and pummeling the roof. There was water, wine, juice and blood everywhere, deadly sharp pieces of glass having flown in all directions and into Sister Kathérine's face.

She was found semi-conscious. A villager pulled her out of the back seat and others helped place her on the ground, attempting to brush away the shards of broken glass without getting cut themselves. They pulled off pieces of their clothing to clear away debris and treat the wounds. Everyone pitched in to help, the truck driver too, as they called for help and continued to apply pieces of clothing to contain Sister Kathérine's bleeding.

Just before sunset, another Peugeot drove by on its way north, emptied its passengers who gently installed Sister Kathérine where they'd once been sitting. She was hastily transported back to Lomé for medical attention. Most of the helpers doubted that she'd survive the ride south. But she did and the new Peugeot driver delivered the groaning, half conscious nun to the hospital near midnight.

The details of the terrible accident were first reported to the nuns by Félix, who repeated the story over and over to add parts he'd omitted and perhaps to assuage his terrible guilt. Then, one by one, the nuns told me the story, each emphasizing a different frightening aspect of the ill-fated journey north. After news of the accident reached the larger community, people in town, at school, passing through could talk of little else. "What a terrible shock!" they wailed to each other, holding hands, shaking their heads and clucking in disapproval of the truck's excessive speed and La Soeur Directrice's fate. It seemed the town was in mourning.

Immediately after the accident, when it was not clear Sister Katherine would recover, all of us at school had a terrible mixture of feelings: guilt for so disliking her combined with overwhelming sympathy for the severity of her injuries. We prayed for her, we sang for her, we wrote beautifully-illustrated get-well letters to her. We did all these things because the nuns and human compassion and the Catholic Church required such gestures. But we also felt a certain calmness with her absence. She wasn't at the school filling us with dread, making us feel on edge and inadequate. I was ashamed of the relief I felt and made up for it by hoping desperately that she'd recover.

We learned that if and when she could travel, she'd be flown to France where better medical resources would be available, hopefully cure the infections, render the headaches less frequent, and guide her to walk again. We would dutifully follow her progress. Would she return to Africa? Surely not. I thought about how terribly mean she'd been with the students. I was certain that if she were fortunate enough to recover, she would become a gentler person. I passionately hoped for both outcomes.

Generally, when a Togolese uses the word family, he is referring to a larger group of relatives than the father, mother, sisters and brothers. The Togolese family includes the grandparents, the parents, the children and all the other relatives such as first, second and third cousins, aunts and uncles. The tie between members of this extended family is very strong.

—PEACE CORPS TRAINING MATERIALS, *"The Togolese Family," Francis Toffa*

FAMILY

UNDER THE PALL of Sister Kathérine's accident, the end of the school year approached slowly and with a great deal of worry and restlessness. La Soeur Directrice continued in serious condition but we learned that she would survive. Three of the nuns had scurried to her side in Lomé. The rest of us were doing our best to fill in, but our performance was lackluster and morale was low. Most of my time in class was taken up with administering tests, distributing answer sheets, handing out exams, and making sure students couldn't look on each others' papers.

"Read the directions carefully!" I warned students. "Take your time and proofread! Keep your eyes on your own work." After one last sweep of the classroom to glare at students in my attempt to prevent cheating, I returned to my desk. This was nun-like teaching behavior I'd adopted, insincerely delivered. Students cooperated to help each other. It's not cheating! I muttered to myself in their defense. I played the role the nuns had modeled, but I shuddered at such unfriendly authoritarianism. And I found the emphasis on exams unfair, hostile, even though I'd known from the beginning that schools in Togo, as well as much of West Africa, followed the draconian French education system.

Between tests, the students and I more or less completed the lessons in the English textbooks, wrapped up the final art project—more stationery—and pushed through to the late 19th century in West African history. These decades were terribly bleak for much of Africa and my presentation of relentless exploitation by western powers depressed me. *C'est vraiment déprimant,* I complained to André. I knew there was more than the textbook account of history, but I felt neither qualified nor permitted to add to it. I persuaded myself to just teach the facts as they were presented—dates and people. Don't editorialize! Besides, I had to prepare students for the end-of-term test.

In the midst of this internal back-and-forth it occurred to me that I might be able to make history more relevant and more concrete by sharing the tapestry that hung on the wall in my living room. I'd bought the cloth as a souvenir during an early visit to the neighboring country of Dahomey. Its brightly colored objects, all weapons, were hand-appliquéd onto a red background. They revealed the history of Abomey, a village near the sea whose leaders had fended off invasion from 1610 to 1900. For three centuries the region was autonomous! Presenting the little-known and heroic struggle represented by this cloth was an effort to re-engage students in our humdrum and textbook-bound review for the end-of-the-year exam. I rolled up the cloth and carted it to history class one morning.

"*Regardez-bien, mes elèves!*" I invited students to approach the front of the room and look carefully at the tapestry. Together we noted the shapes of weapons, guns, knives, and swords, and I explained how each pair of symbols corresponded to one of twelve kings who'd ruled straight through three centuries.

"*C'est étonnant, non*?!" I tried to generate awe and curiosity in this representation of unity, resistance, self-determination, but clearly I seemed more interested in this bit of local history than my students did. I encouraged them to ask questions, but since these girls had not been taught to question or perhaps, lacked interest, it took much prodding and modeling. Finally, we made a list of what more we wanted to know about the history revealed in the cloth. "Why didn't other villages resist invasion? Was Lama-Kara invaded? Were Europeans the only invaders? Didn't Africans take part in the slave trade? How was Abomey finally defeated?" The girls appeared mildly motivated to learn more, and I finally felt ok about a history lesson.

In PE, the students and I approached the end of our fitness campaign. I led them in ten laps around the soccer field and we met our goal of completing twenty-five jumping jacks without stopping.

"*Sautez! Suivez! Vous êtes fortes jeunes filles!*" I called to the girls as they ran around the field, commending them for their increased endurance. "Single file now! Don't slow down, Hélène! Heads up! Knees high! You all look great!" I was proud of their improvement and ability to follow my directions in English. Would they ever use the English they'd learned? Even on the field when they were most engaged, the students seemed distracted. They definitely concentrated less on homework, were fidgety in class and didn't seem to mind if their test scores were low. I echoed their detachment.

A teaching routine (mostly) mastered and a (mostly) comfortable and familiar life left me restless. Part of me was anxious to return home. But extending my stay in Togo, after I'd finally figured out how to survive and even thrive, was enticing. I wrote one letter home claiming, "Just last weekend I decided to stay in Togo for a third year! Everything will be soooo much easier." In the next letter, I described my restlessness.

"Oh, I'm so tired of teaching. I feel useless these days and am ready to come home." Did I need to always be seeking? Struggling on the edge of a new adventure? For the first time in two years, in an effort to stimulate re-engagement, I permitted students to visit me at my home. The nuns would never have approved, but I suppose I was desperate.

"Pleeeease continue at Collège Adèle," they pleaded as we posed for pictures in the shade of my banana tree. I stood surrounded by a semi-circle of stunningly beautiful young women, each decked out in a brightly colored dress or a traditional outfit for this visit. Click! We shifted to another photo pose in two rows, hands on our knees and heads up, feeling silly and smiling broadly. Click!

"Let's be crazy!" Evangéline called out and we stood, wrapping our arms around each other, making funny faces. Laughing and promising to make copies of the photos, I told the girls that I'd stay in Togo for a third year though I wasn't sure I'd be teaching at Collège Adèle.

"I have to learn to teach boys!" I confessed to them.

"Oh, boys are <u>much</u> easier than we've been, *Mees*. You don't need to learn a thing to teach boys. We need you! You can really teach us. You make us want to learn!" I was surprised and delighted to hear what they said. Our photographer for the visit was Arsène, my boy for the last several months. He was wise beyond his twelve years and, like Sina and Florent, my previous *boys*, helped me with everything from servicing my motorbike to going to market and cooking. I had to agree that he'd been much easier to teach than my female students. The girls had a point.

Arsène came from a large family outside of town. Number five of nine children, he went to school at Collège Chaminade, the boys' partner to Collège Adèle. Arsène longed to learn English faster than his grammar

Arsène (on the left) with his family

teacher made possible and he wanted to contribute to what his family paid for his school supplies and uniform, so he was thrilled to work for me and earn a small sum of money.

I adored Arsène. Each afternoon I taught him a new song or rhyme, which he memorized immediately and taught everyone in his family that same day. Always smiling, he was so eager to help me, replanting flower seeds after the chickens had pecked them out of the small bed, disposing of an unfortunate bird the cat had brought inside, washing dishes and dusting the sandy shelves. During one long weekend I took him to Lomé on the train like I'd done with Sina, my very first boy, exposing him too to sights and sounds and crowds he could never have imagined. He was so appreciative of my mentoring and I was so grateful, once again, to have a helper I could trust. I attempted to explain this to his parents on a weekend visit to their home.

"*Maman, vous ne pouvez pas imaginer comment j'apprécie votre fils.*" I talked to his mother who was surprisingly vibrant after bearing nine children. I explained how much I'd come to rely on Arsène. But her French and my Kabré were too limited for us to really have a conversation. Arsène and Bernard, an older sibling, took turns translating. Through their filter of modesty, my gushing became a simple statement of gratefulness. Maman nodded. I met brothers and sisters and cousins and aunts and uncles and observed how this large family was its own high functioning community. The children hastened from task to task, all in their best clothes, school uniforms, for my visit. They stayed mostly silent and busy, staring at me with wide curious eyes, then averting them quickly when I caught their gazes.

"*N'ayez pas peur!*" I discouraged their coyness and tried to get them to approach me. Arsène's nine-year-old brother coached a six-year-old sister to hand me a Coke. "*Merci!*" I said. She smiled shyly then ran back to hide in the pagne folds of an older sister's skirt. Big sister was surveying the scene while stirring a pot of aromatic fish stew.

The family compound was just outside of town. It consisted of a row of rooms that opened to a bare concrete platform. Fragrant Eucalyptus trees surrounded the living space. Papa sat in a chair surrounded by neighbors and family members, some standing but most sitting on the cement. Male adults chatted while everyone else, Maman and children of all ages, worked. Eventually, all of us sat on the platform in two circles, *Papa*, Uncle and me in one circle and Maman and all of the children in another. We dipped round mounds of fufu into large bowls and I found the stew as delectable as the togetherness. This was a dream for me, this family.

By now I was accustomed to men eating separately from women and children, and was reassured that at least we were eating at the same time, instead of in two phases when it could feel as if the women and children were getting leftovers. On this afternoon, after our meal together, we posed for a photo, Papa in the center on the chair, Maman standing on one side and me on the other. Everyone else was arranged by height. I counted twenty-three people, ranging in age from a few months to 60-something. It was unusual to find such a large family, so many children, from the same mother and father. Large families with many children were common, but so were several wives. I marveled at the respect and cooperation Arsène's family members showed each other, and I was happy to be a part of their afternoon and Arsène's life.

"Théodore, Angélique, Marianne, Matthieu," I went around the circle trying to memorize everyone's name. By the end of the visit Maman and Papa and the older children knew the names of my family members, assuming that close family relationships were universal, extending beyond northern Togo. I made a promise to myself to nurture this kind of family closeness when I returned home.

Before we parted, Arsène had his family recite "Here is a Church, Here is the Steeple," hand gestures and all. They also sang "Row, Row, Row Your Boat" for me. "Merrily" came out "May-heh-lee" for most of the singers, but I thought there was a good chance Arsène would become a teacher. I'd made a contribution to the future of Togolese education.

"Good-bye! Merci!" I called out, walking down the path that led out of the compound, escorted by a flank of children carrying my bag and a few modest gifts. They walked me all the way to the main road and waved goodbye. Few of my American friends had been invited to such an intimate family meal. I felt so lucky. This is what I'd wanted all along, not to be mistaken for a local but to immerse myself comfortably in local life, warmly accepted. How deeply rewarding it had been to experience the love and trust of this sweet family.

The world is like he skin of the chameleon. It changes fast.

— **MIMI ROBINSON**, *Still It Makes Me Laugh:*
Impressions of West Africa

GOODBYE LAMA-KARA?
GOODBYE TOGO?

IT WAS RAINING almost every day now. Unpredictable showers made everything messy. As I walked about town completing errands, my legs got splattered with mud. I zoomed to school on my mobylette and dismounted, noting how the rivulets of water wove a criss-cross pattern across the tops of my dusty sandaled feet. Although it was the last month of classes, I still hadn't decided whether to stay in Togo or

With Peace Corps staff—Christian is on my left

return to the U.S. I sketched out a T-chart, similar to the one I'd done two years earlier when my initial aversion to the capital city of Lomé had me questioning a commitment to stay faraway for such a long time. Once again, I attempted to put reason over longing.

Reasons to Stay in Togo	Reasons to Go Home
• *reap benefit of 2 years' learning and apply all I've learned to easier living abroad* • *have more fun* • *save money* • *finish macramé and sewing projects* • *stick with Polly* • *not leave André*	• *be with my family and FRIENDS* • *eat all the food I've missed*

As before, the chart determined that I stay.

"I put in a request for an English teaching position at a large coed school in the south!" I told Polly, hoping to teach alongside Togolese colleagues rather than the solitary European nuns who shared so little. And I was ready for the more common challenges of teaching huge coed classes. I was sure it wouldn't be as bad as what I'd experienced during the previous year's visit to a local high school. I needed to expand my experience! I saw now, more clearly than ever, that I'd been lucky to land at Collège

Ste. Adèle. Casting aside the curtain of Catholicism, the clean classrooms, small classes, sufficient textbooks and high academic expectations had actually allowed me to teach. Well, most of the time. My friends in other more typical schools hadn't had it so good. I could handle large chaotic classes now after two years' training at Adèle, I muttered to myself, half hopeful, half determined to try to take on something new and different. And as for everything else, it felt like I deserved some time to capitalize on two years' learning. Now that I moved about like a local, switched languages as I changed regions and tasks, life seemed much easier. "It takes a full two years to get used to this life," I repeated to Polly, "to feel at home." She cheerfully agreed. *"L'Afrique—c'est une question d'habitude."* Yes, it really did take time to get to know Africa.

But when not hastening to defend a third year in Togo, I ached with longing to return home and be with friends and family. I missed my stepmama's quirkiness, my mother's inextinguishable faith in me, and my sister's gardening magic. I felt so out of touch. My copies of *Time Magazine* came late and wrinkled with handling, and did little to answer my questions about current events. I knew the headlines: there was peace in Vietnam and the Supreme Court had ruled abortion a constitutional right. But I was hungry for news as it was happening, more nuanced interpretations, details. I also craved hamburgers from our local drive-through, Eat 'N Run, and the sweet and crumbly coffee cake mix we made on weekend mornings. I'd become impatient with hours that stretched into days, weeks and months. I missed steady urgency, busy-ness, hustle and bustle. While I was proud of my ability to flow with the languor of village life, I often wanted more to do. I began to have more frequent dreams of being surrounded by people from my past. And although André and I had reached a deep level of affection for one other, there was an uncomfortable and unspoken queasiness about the limitations of our romance, at least on my part. He'd said often that we weren't made to be married. I never agreed because, I suppose, the only way I could justify a relationship at all was by claiming that it was for forever. I wasn't a casual dater, or at least didn't want to be one. Yet my actions weren't consistent with my insistence, spoken and unspoken, that we were sweethearts for life. Perhaps, without admitting this to myself, I agreed with André.

I'd sent several requests for work in the States, not expecting anything to materialize with a scarcity of stateside jobs and the six-week mail turn-around. Money, jobs, and happiness were too hard to achieve in California. So after vacillating for many months, my decision to stay in Togo was a relief. That's what I told myself. I'd made myself a fine home here. Declaring an end to this period of indecision, I paid closer attention to what was now expected and familiar, features of everyday life. Walking around town I came upon a pop-up soccer match. The players were boys, always only boys. My students were girls, always only girls. I definitely needed to branch out and get a feeling for male students in Year #3.

"*Ouf!*" I exclaimed, caught in the path of a flying soccer ball. The boys ran toward the ball and me. "*Excusez! Excusez!*" they shouted and recoiled, exchanging embraces and embarrassed smiles.

"*Pas de problème,*" I replied, picking up the ball, noting that it was made of crumpled paper tightly wadded, beginning to shed its outer layer. I tossed back the dusty sphere with its trailing tail to a chorus of "*mercis!*" Children here were inventive with more than soccer balls. They created intricate toys with wheels from pieces of tin cans and wire that they pushed along dirt pathways with six-foot bamboo poles. But it was

Testing their wire wagon

their ready willingness to play together that was most remarkable to me. They traded turns without conflict or competition. I'd watched the kids in my compound help each other sweep, refill the oil lamps, catch chickens, care for babies, carry wood, water, ignams, bags of rice, cloth and fuel. Their eagerness to assist, happily and ably, continued to amaze me.

My fascination with peer and family dynamics in Togo motivated many conversations with André. Since our first evening together, now nearly two years ago, I'd been hearing about his beloved grandma. I'd become convinced she was responsible for teaching him so much of what I cherished about her grandson: his *politesse*, respect, tenderness and sensitivity. "*C'est Mamavie, la reine de la famille,*" André said often. Mamavie was the beloved "queen" of the family. For months he'd been hoping to take me to his grandmother's village in the south, east of Lomé. Finally, as there'd been too much talk about my possible departure, he secured time off from work, arranged transportation and granted Mamavie's repeated requests to welcome us.

"*N'oublies pas, Bubu,*" André warned me about communication challenges as we headed south together, "*Mamavie ne parle pas tes langues.*" He said that though both *Mamavie* and I spoke several languages, they were not the same.

"*Et en plus,*" he added, "*elle ne connais pas des yovos!*" She'd never spent time with yovos, white people, foreigners. I knew all of this, of course, but instead of dampening my enthusiasm, the reminder was exhilarating. I was working my way into intimate family relationships, building trust, learning and showing that no matter who we are, where we come from, what we do, how we speak, we were all human. I could hardly wait.

After a train, bus and taxi ride, we arrived at the village and began walking to Mamavie's compound. I couldn't decide which was more thrilling: traveling with André or finally getting to visit Mamavie. Doing both of these was beyond my wildest dreams. I was alert with delight. I followed André's lead on a network of narrow dirt paths, serpentining through fields and watching a group of young men bent over their neatly arranged mounds of ignams. The sun's brightness radiated off their smooth bare backs as they worked the soil. I hastened along, breathing in the fresh earthy smells, trying not to lose my footing on the soft edges of the narrow pathway. Rows of lacey manioc bushes bordered each field and the patterns and textures distracted me. We met villagers twice, coming the opposite direction, and paused while André greeted them and gave a quick update on our visit to Mamavie. I nodded and smiled and shook hands with everyone, adults first, then youngsters, as they deposited their loads to free their hands to greet us. The villagers were so friendly. Their enthusiasm fed my euphoria.

We approached Mamavie's compound and three children ran toward us, grabbing our bags of oranges, bread, potatoes and packets of dried fish. We proceeded to Mamavie's hut. Bending nearly in half to enter, we took a minute to let our eyes adjust from the dazzling sunlight to the darkness of a small, cool room. I smelled ash, spent fires. One by one, the objects in Mamavie's living space appeared. First, Mamavie. She was seated on a wooden bench draped in a pattern of lime green and turquoise pagnes, one for a skirt, a second for a shawl and a third wrapped around her head. We caught her in a reverie as we entered. She pulled herself upright and her dark face brightened. I noted how tiny she was. She raised both arms in delight as André walked towards her. They held each other, he leaning, she reaching, for several minutes. André was more beautiful, more gracious and deferential than I'd ever seen him, reluctant to let go of Mamavie's arms.

"*Bubu! Mamavie!*" he said, talking to both of us at the same time, alerting one and introducing the other. I approached and followed André's lead again, taking Mamavie's arms, and smiling until my cheeks hurt. I'd earned this moment. Bubu loved me enough to introduce me to his beloved grandmother and share her home.

We attempted a few polite greetings, but I couldn't go very far with language. Our nonverbal exchanges were more effective. I took a seat next to Mamavie on the bench and put my arm through her elbow and wove my fingers into hers. Like this we sat while she and André talked, catching each other up on harvest predictions, neighbor events, family milestones. I studied the objects in Mamavie's living space: baskets of dried fish, cans of oil, a small tray of fresh tomatoes and a stack of folded clothing. There was a tower of calabashes too, one resting inside another, forming a simple sculpture of round shapes, smooth surfaces and light brown colors.

"*Elle parle du maïs,*" André explained that they were talking about this season's corn crop. "*Elle parle aussi de son bonheur de notre visite.*" And of her happiness at our visit. I eased into a dreamy calm, drinking in this intimacy. I didn't remember ever feeling so full. I squeezed Mamavie's small bony hand. André continued to loop me into the conversations every so often, translating a question then an answer or explaining what he'd just said.

"*Mamavie dit que tu es très adorable et gentille.*" I redirected the compliments back to Mamavie. "C'est elle," I said. She was the sweet, adorable one. When she finally addressed me directly in her native language of *Mina*, she asked how long I'd be in Togo. André translated and we laughed, marking shared relief at my recent decision to stay for another year. He told her I'd be here for a while longer. They continued talking as I sat silently, awed and envious of this grandmother-grandson tenderness. I'd never had a relationship with my grandparents. Of those who'd lived long enough for me to know, one was disapproving and punitive, the other dismissed those who were different. I never knew a grandma could be so loving, care so sincerely about a grandchild's well-being. Maybe I'd stay in Togo forever. Maybe I'd make Togo my permanent home. I felt immediately guilty at this thought and the idea of abandoning my mom.

Looking out the small entrance of Mamavie's home, I saw children sweeping, women with babies on their backs pounding fufu, and teens tending fires and carrying water. It was all so familiar. About an hour into the visit, we sat on the smooth earth floor and were served fufu and spicy tomato sauce, rolling the steaming white balls in our fingers to cool them before plopping them in our mouths, then breathing through our teeth for relief from the temperature and the spiciness.

"*Bon appétit! Bon appétit!*" we chorused. André and I ate heartily and encouraged Mamavie to keep up with us. She chuckled.

The afternoon moved to evening in slow motion. Mamavie sat noiselessly and took us in. André dozed after eating while I wondered about

Mamavie's ability to be so serene. I wondered about what beyond seeing her grandson made her happy. She was so peaceful, so untroubled. We caught each other's glimpses throughout the afternoon, short furtive glances full of curiosity. We smiled. My cheeks would be aching for days from so much smiling.

When it was time to leave, we hustled about the compound shaking hands, communicating our appreciation, gathering spices, two pagnes and a basket of mangoes Mamavie had prepared for us. For the first time Mamavie walked outside, shading her eyes from the bright sun, and made her way to the path that led out of the compound. She was solid on her feet, but slow. André embraced her for a long time and then turned aside to usher me into the good-bye ritual. I put my arms around Mamavie, holding her small strong body in an awkward hug. When we detached I saw that there were tears in her eyes and I squeezed her small hands.

"Oh, *Bubu*! *Il faut retourner!*" As we walked away, I begged André to come back soon and bring me along. He promised a return visit and we continued, turning and waving every five feet. When we were finally out of sight, I began to cry, silently, overcome with emotion and reverence for Mamavie's love of her grandson and for his love of her. André took my hand, leading me away from the village and back toward the car park. After a long silence, I told him how grateful I was to have made this visit with him.

"*Toi-là*," I said. "*Tu es tellement chanceux. Ta Mamavie est formidable.*" He was lucky; I was grateful. And I was exhausted from the tender emotions and intimacy of the afternoon.

We caught a bush taxi and headed to Lomé planning to spend a couple of days in the city before heading north again. I sat close to André, squeezing his strong fleshy hand, feeling so taken care of by this sweet generous man. I relaxed into him as we bumped along in the taxi, anchoring my body in his steadiness. I tried hard to hold onto Mamavie's tenderness as we were jolted back to city life—the relentless honking of horns, the dust, the crowds and smells that offered a mixture of sewage and sea. We made the transition from village to city silently, then settled into an evening of closeness. I felt so much love.

We made the most of our two days in the capital, adapting to the swift pace, the crowds, the opportunities that didn't exist elsewhere. I visited Soeur Kathérine in the hospital, still bedridden, but able to recognize me and speak softly. I felt a sudden wave of kindness toward her. André and I visited the beach, ate at a popular German brasserie, took a walk through the emerging European neighborhood and stopped at Edith's Inn, where it felt, finally, that Edith and I were truly happy to see one another. This had been my first home in Africa, I reflected. I was so happy to realize that I felt light years away from those uncomfortable early days.

"There's a letter waiting for you at the office," she told me. "A Peace Corps staff member came by the inn to ask your whereabouts. Hurry over and pick up your mail before they take it north on a delivery run," Edith advised.

At the Peace Corps office, André and I spent time greeting the staff we hadn't seen for a while. They were busy preparing for a new group of construction volunteers. I collected my mail which included a rolled up

Time Magazine, only three weeks old, and a few letters from home. One, notably, was from Robie, a name I'd heard but a person I'd never met. She was my aunt's roommate from college currently directing an education program on the Navajo Indian Reservation in Arizona. She wrote that she was desperate to hire someone with experience in teaching English learners. "Your Aunt Connie tells me you've been teaching in Africa. I need a Specialist in English as a Second Language (ESL) to begin work here next month. Would you consider this?" The typewritten words got blurry as I was at first thrilled with the job offer, then almost immediately jolted back to the grim possibility of not staying in Togo. A specialist in my third year of teaching? It seemed both preposterous and fabulous. I felt a pit in my stomach, helpless about a decision that seemed already to have been made. A job on the Navajo Reservation seemed a much better option than a Togolese public high school instructor.

"Oh my gosh! *Bubu!*" I shouted at reading the letter, interrupting his animated conversation with Etienne, one of the Peace Corps language teachers. "I can't believe this! I have a job offer in the States!" I showed André the letter and felt a mixture of exhilaration, nervousness, fear, and urgency. How could I turn this down? Should I accept this and move to Arizona? Or should I stay in Togo? I worried that a third year in Togo would so strengthen my attachment to this place that I'd never go home. How could I ever leave? I read the letter again. I'd be teaching English to small groups of Navajo-speaking students, from kindergarten-age to high school. What a great opportunity—all ages, boys and girls! I didn't think I could turn it down. I'd take the job, see my mom, brother, sister, dad, stepmom and friends and come back to Togo! Yes. I could do it all. I'd take the job and come back.

André listened. He looked at me and raised his eyebrows, a familiar gesture that usually meant, "It's up to you. It wouldn't matter what I'd say anyway."

"*Bubu, fais ce qu'il faut. Je t'attendrais.*" André advised me to do what I had to do. He'd wait for my return. I was approaching my mid-twenties and didn't know what to ask of him. Could I ask him to wait for me? Didn't he plan to marry after my departure? Didn't I want to be free to date others? Not really capable of suggesting he marry or even date others, I begged him to wait for me. Selfish girl. I wanted it all—André's faithfulness <u>and</u> job opportunities!

"*Oui, Bubu. It faut rentrer et revenir. Je serais la!*" André said that I needed to accept this opportunity, visit my family and return. I was always surprised when he was able to put my needs before his. I'd never been able to do that for another.

In the day that followed I had conversations with friends and spent mostly sleepless nights. I recognized that the public high school position in the south of Togo that hadn't been secured lost its luster in light of the Navajo opportunity. Buoyed by André's support, the advice of my friends and my pressing desire to justify going home, I resolved to return to the States, accept Robie's contract offer and return, eventually, to Togo. So, hastily, I prepared to leave.

"*Çe n'est pas pour toujours,*" I told André over and over, talking more to myself than to him. It wasn't for forever.

We traveled north for the last time together. I rushed through a series of good-byes to friends, students, my beloved kitty. I zoomed around to my favorite shopkeepers and market vendors and told them I was leaving, but I'd be back. For all of them, I made big promises to greet each of my family members on their behalf, for by now they knew everyone's name.

I was leaving Togo two months short of two years. It was so scary. Did I know anything about teaching English? It was so risky. What would become of André and me? It was so swift. I had two weeks to gather up two years and leave. I stayed busy and avoided thinking about what it all meant. Quickly I assembled of list of tasks: order a new dress, buy some gift gourd-rattles, look for more brass figurines. Prepare your trunk, get the mailing addresses of Elise, Elizabeth, Michel. Don't forget the letters volunteers have asked you to mail from the States.

The final days were a whirlwind. I gave away kitchen items to compound mates, passed on my collection of books and cassette tapes to the new volunteers. I said goodbye to the nuns at Collège Adèle promising to send them school supplies, and gifted cushions from my makeshift living room couch to Herbert and Dada and their children. I closed the front door of my living space, said goodbye to flowering impatiens in the tiny garden, shook the small hands of each of the children lined up to bid farewell, and headed south again with bags and suitcase. André and Polly planned to meet me in Lomé and escort me to the Ghana border. I felt more excitement than regret. I was eager to be off on a new adventure and the restlessness that had been so much of my life for the last few months seemed to be momentarily tamed. Driving away from Lama-Kara, I peered out at the fields turning green with the recent rains, plants growing taller and stronger with new life.

I tried to keep my goodbyes with Polly and André unceremonious. I knew I'd see them again and repeatedly reassured them of this, though Arizona seemed farther away to them than it did to me. We spent my last week in Lomé together, making African cloth purchases at the market, packing up the trunk I was sending home and saying goodbye to Peace Corps staff and friends. We went dancing each night and then walked along the beach, pushed forward by a warm wind under a sky full of stars. I vowed to remember the feel of the warm beach breeze, the noises of the traffic and even the smells of the city, once so odious and now so familiar. I tried to take memory photographs of our synchronized moves on the dance floor, Polly's ebullient smiles and André's tender hold. When I got too caught up in emotions of the moment, fear, regret, anticipation, hastiness, I stopped and breathed in Mamavie's serenity. My heart felt full when I thought of her.

On the last day my two good friends escorted me to the Ghana customs office. Polly looked longingly at me, regularly letting out loud sighs. André greeted border patrol colleagues and made sure my passport got stamped correctly, my bags got passed through swiftly, and a reliable taxi driver appeared to take me to the airport. I would miss both of these friends who'd been loyal through such an unforgettable two years. I felt like a numb actor moving through a series of ritualized gestures and promises, playing these moments cheerfully, refusing to acknowledge that this moment and these friends were the end of a hard-earned dream life. Once again I was leaving one home for another. The hastened departure cast a veil of rosy happiness over memories of the last two years.

"I'll keep you informed of everything going on here," Polly promised, as she'd decided to stay another year.

"*Ecris souvent!*" André implored me to write often.

"*Oui—tous les jours!* Every day!" I promised.

We exchanged long hugs several times, holding onto each other until the taxi driver shouted.

"*Mademoiselle! On va partir!*" Clinging to André's arm then wrist then fingers, I released my hold and stumbled to the taxi. I was really leaving.

"*A bientot!*" we called to each other with hopeful certainty as I proceeded across the border and into the cab. My friends disappeared behind the small barricade. "I love you both! See you soooooon!"

Going home is easy. The hard part is what happens after you arrive.

—**EKOW ESHUN**, *Black Gold of the Sun: Searching for Home in England and Africa*

EPILOGUE: HOME

I **RETURNED TO SAN FRANCISCO** after a series of flights that dropped me midway between terrible angst and a northern California summer. The sky was clear, the air was warm and the prospect of finally reconnecting with friends and family distracted me from thinking about what I'd left behind. Did I make the right decision? Should I have just come home for vacation? Should I have stayed in Togo? The reunion with

Climbing Mount Kilimanjaro 1974

my mom caught us giddy and tearful. I was relieved to find her busy planning classroom projects for the school year and dreaming up bulletin board displays with enthusiasm rather than dread. She appeared healthy. I didn't probe deeply, hoping that alcohol had weakened its pull on her lonely evenings.

I acted out my homecoming, playing it elated, celebratory, totally committed to the relocation I'd made. But behind the scenes I wasn't so sure. Most of the time I ached with regret, nostalgia, and longing. The gifts I doled out to friends and family kept me focused on a past life. I lavished custom-made clothes of striking African fabric on my stepmom and dad. We three paraded into their local country club dressed in billowing African outfits. My father presented me to the golf pro and my stepmom regaled the restaurant manager with details of where I'd been.

"Togo?! Don't they specialize in sandwiches?" Few people seemed aware that Togo was a country in Africa. Those who didn't associate the country's name with a sandwich chain thought it referred to an island in the South Pacific.

"Are you thinking of Tonga?" I asked, resolving to build African geography into any further teaching I'd do.

My sister and I reconnected by phone on her drive south from Oregon to welcome me home. I read and reread my brother's most recent aerogram. He was in Australia now, having traveled almost all the way around the world. I took heart in our shared dreams to travel but lamented that those inclinations continued to separate us. My friends hosted an enthusiastic welcome home reception, still marveling at my ability to have stayed away so long.

"You're so thin!"

"You're so tan!"

"You haven't changed a bit!"

But I felt radically changed and disappointed that everything at home had stayed the same. I was tormented by great longing for André, my students, my life in Lama-Kara. I continued having weird dreams, though I'd stopped taking malaria medicine. I spent hours sitting cross-legged on my mother's worn living room carpet listening to the cassette tapes of African music André had compiled for me and demonstrated to my mom favorite dance moves. She could manage some of the footwork but the hip wiggling was quite beyond her. We laughed together at her efforts. I wrote letters to people I missed in Togo, decorating stationery with Charlie Brown stickers, way less artistic than the designs my students had sketched and colored. And I read and reread letters with the flowery handwriting and address lines in all the wrong places that had miraculously made their way to my California address.

It was physically painful, my longing. Something from within my gut gnawed, from my lower back to my belly. I felt nervous and empty, lost, disoriented, adrift. People continued to ask questions about what I'd done in Togo, what I'd eaten, whom I'd met. I didn't have words for my confusion and my play-acting didn't leave room for such complicated feelings. So I hosted slideshows and tried to make the life I'd led so far away familiar to them. To my disappointment and alarm, everyone was much more interested in the present and future. Their questions moved swiftly from then to now:

"What will you do now?" from Carol, a childhood friend.

"Arizona? Navajo Indians? Any similarities to Africans? Where is Rough Rock? It seems as far away as Togo!" asked Sylvia, my mom's pal.

At the end of two weeks in northern California, attempting closure on nearly two years in Togo, my mom, sis and I piled into the baby blue Toyota for the drive to Arizona. If I kept moving, the *malaise* I felt could be held at bay. We made brief stops to visit people from the past, dropping in to see my friend from Lama-Kara, my high school sweetheart who had briefly been my husband, and my former boyfriend from Ghana who had fast-forwarded his career to a management position in a financial company. The visits linked together disparate pieces of my life like a hand-sewn quilt, putting previous, current and future up against each other through raw edges and rough seams. At journey's end, mental and physical angst decelerated, I found myself settling into a small home on the Navajo Reservation with my local housemate Louise Begay, preparing to teach at an independent Navajo school. Bees collected powdery pollen from the tall pink hollyhocks that framed the front door. The breeze blew hot, dry and empty.

Adjustment to life on the Navajo Reservation was rocky. The contrasts between Togolese and Navajos were too vast for me to bridge in the early months. Where Africans had been loud, friendly, and curious, the Native Americans I encountered cast their eyes downward and spoke in whispers. They lived miles apart from one another, unlike my African acquaintances who lived in crowded communal compounds with three or four other families. I did my best to make new friends with a random assortment of teachers, missionaries, activists and Louise's many siblings. I took lessons in Navajo, *Yá'át'ééh!*, relished Navajo Fry Bread and was happy as an ESL Specialist, teaching boys and learning to work with small groups. I struggled to make my African wardrobe work in the snow—it didn't—and to perfect *la sauce d'arachide*, peanut stew, with Skippy's Crunchy. I hiked, obtained a teacher's credential through correspondence courses and played with watercolors, attempting to capture the shades of the desert. Although the serenity of the region calmed me, I looked frequently at one of Arsène's drawings scotch-taped to my bedroom wall: un collier, a small necklace, complete with gris-gris pouch, to keep me well and help me thrive in my new home.

Most of the time I dreamed of Togo. I made sense of it all by theorizing that immersion in one's first foreign culture captures our allegiance. So in an apologetic conversation with my supervisor I asked to cut my two-year contract short. This came as no surprise to Robie who wished me well. Perhaps she knew all along that I'd be leaving early.

As soon as the school year ended, I flew back to Togo, just as I'd promised my pals. In the year I'd been away, the Togolese president had launched an *authenticité* campaign, a return to indigenous values. Names of towns and holidays had been changed, traditional clothing had been reintroduced and symbols of European colonialism had been obscured. André, now FoKodjo, was the same tender generous man, but he seemed shorter, smaller, more provincial in his new identity. I felt uneasy. Immediately folded into a new Peace Corps training program, teaching in Togo seemed limited, too restricted. I traveled to Lama-Kara, now called Kara, to visit former students and the nuns, who reported that Sister Katherine was slowly recovering in France. I felt detached with the ubiquitous changes. During the year in Arizona, in spite of the early discomfort I'd felt, my world had expanded. Initial resistance to new people and places had become a familiar phenomenon. Now back in Togo, this wasn't the place I'd left behind and spent a year inflating in my dreams. Moreover, I was no longer the novice teacher, eager Peace Corps volunteer who had found everything, or many things, so magical. So I decided to push on. As it had been in California, my return visit to Togo was brief. I staged another round of goodbyes, this time more reconciled to a departure. This time good-byes were easier and André and I parted loving friends, with his plans to marry soon and mine to travel. Accompanied by Polly and Lynn, another Peace Corps friend, I took a month to explore East Africa. From the top of Kilimanjaro we peered down beyond the clouds to the vastness of what was visible of the land and sea. The climb paralleled my time in Togo: magnificent, grueling, painful, triumphant.

Finally, I flew to America and hopped on a train that would take me, slowly, from Florida to Arizona. This was the first opportunity I'd had in many months to sit still, to reflect on the past several years and think about my life as a young woman and my place in the world. My experiences had stretched my curiosity rather than quelled it. I felt I had learned something big, something profound about the world and the people in it. I had learned to accept, even respect what I'd renounced earlier. I'd seen the universe in my small West African community. Differences were not obstacles to respect and affection. I vowed to keep moving, to use the past as a vehicle for moving forward rather than as a shelter to help me feel secure. Over the course of the train ride with its intermittent stops and restarts. I thought back to my impulsive reaction to Edith and how much I'd changed by the time I visited André's grandmother. I was much more comfortable with the unknown. I'd come to realize that home wasn't a place, a certain kind of family, a fixed professional role, or an established and protective ring of friends. It had to be a gentle urgency and quiet confidence in my seeking—trusting that each choice despite the inevitable waves of distress, anxiety and exclusion would carry me forward to a sense, no matter how fleeting, of home.

ACKNOWLEDGEMENTS

When you've been working on a project for as long as I have, there are many people to thank. The initial call to tell my story came from UC Berkeley's Bay Area Writing Project and I will always be grateful. The on-going support of BAWP colleagues through workshops, writing groups and helpful conversations shaped and refined each tale. Marty Williams' monthly gatherings of inspiring and hard-working writers in our Manu-script Writing Group offered examples in their own pieces and feedback for mine that helped me get closer to what I wanted to convey. Boundless gratitude to Mark Ali, David Braden, Page Hersey, Jim Hughes, D. M. Kloker, Grace Morizawa, Charlie Stephens, Carla Williams-Namboodiri, and of course, Marty. Mary Ann Smith's Professional Writing Group offered further direction and inspiration. Stan Pesick, Grace Morizawa, Sandra Murphy, Shelly Weintraub, Laury Fischer and Mary Ann asked questions that helped me link themes and explore meaning more deeply.

Tania Amochaev, Sivani Babu, Sabine Bergman, Tim Cahill, Matthew Felix, Dave Fox, Anette Nyqvist, Meghan Selway, Liz Shemaria and Keith Skinner from Book Passage Travel Writers' Conference were particularly helpful with several chapters. A longstanding group of cherished friends provided encouragement and thoughtful commentary, reflecting their brilliance as writers and as literary luminaries. Marlene Buono, Trish Manwaring, Caitlin Mohan, Kim Roen and Jennifer Sterling escorted this project along with insight and engagement.

Special thanks to Lucia Blakeslee for saving my letters, to John Fanselow, my Peace Corps Trainer, a supreme teaching and learning visionary, to Togo contemporaries Brian Rawlinson, Suzanne Spolarich, Lynn Armstrong and Kelly Morris for their generosity with material and memories. Editors Barbara Gates and Carol Bergman provided perceptive and fruitful feedback. My daughter-in-law, Rebecca Faustine Baky, began the design process with discernment and talent. Peter Pike and David Fielding answered many questions, sometimes more than once, about the complexities of the publishing process. Dyan Pike and Audrey Fielding guided the project along with enthusiasm and practicality. Finally, generous friends read and remarked on the manuscript and improved it with each read. Hearty thanks to Audrey Fielding, Sharon Jones, Bob Pressnall, Alice Gosak, Eileen Hamilton, Patricia Gustafson, Lynn Armstrong, Chris Lyons and Cindy Beams. My gratitude is immeasurable.

GLOSSARY

authenticité	campaign to change names of people and places from European languages to indigenous languages
balançoir	a swing; small metal sculpture that balances a figure or object
bananier	banana tree
Bedouin	Arabic-speaking nomad living in or near the Sahara
beignet	deep fried pastry sprinkled with sugar
blanchisseur	laundryman/woman
boubou	long gown worn by men and women
CFA	currency of 14 countries in Africa
cahier	notebook
calabash	a large spoon or bowl made from a dried and hollowed gourd
citronelle	wild aromatic plant used for tea; its scent deters mosquitoes
collier	necklace
doyen/ne	the person in charge
Francophone	French-speaking
fufu	pounded yam
gris gris	a charm that invites good fortune or prevents evil
harmattan	warm, dry wind that blows from the Sahara November-January
l' heure Africaine	refers lightheartedly to casual sense of time, common in Africa
ignam	large white tuber, plentiful in northern Togo and basis of "fufu"
infirmièr/e	nurse

insupportable	not tolerable
Kotokoli	language of region in and around Sokodé
kuli kuli	sweet peanut candy
lycêe	high school
malaise	discomfort
manguier	mango tree
médecin/e	doctor
militaire	soldier
mobylette	battery and pedal-powered scooter
muezzin	man who calls Muslims to prayer from the minaret of a mosque
pagne	colorful printed, tie-dyed, dyed African cloth, measured in meters
palmier	palm tree
patte	pounded yam, eaten with several varieties of sauce
piment	hot (spicy) pepper
policier	policeman
quaie	boardwalk along the water
raison d'être	purpose
tress	braid, bunch, tie hair
Tuareg	a nomad from a Berber ethnic subgroup living in the vast Sahara region and known for trading animals, jewelry, spices
voleurs	thieves, bandits
yovo	white person/foreigner

BIBLIOGRAPHY

Belcher, Wendy Laura. Honey from the Lion: An African Journey. New York: E. P. Dutton, 1988.

Biddlecombe, Peter. French Lessons in Africa: Travels with my briefcase through French Africa. London: Little, Brown & Company, 1993.

Charles, Laurie L. Intimate Colonialism: Head, Heart & Body in West African Development Work. Walnut Creek, CA.: Left Coast Press, Inc., 2007.

Drew, Eileen. The Ivory Crocodile. Minneapolis: Coffee House Press, 1996.

Eshun, Ekow. Black Gold of the Sun. London: Penguin Books, 2005.

Grinker, Roy Richard. In the Arms of Africa: The Life of Colin M. Turnbull. New York: St. Martin's Press, 2000.

Herrera, Susana. Mango Elephants in the Sun: How Life in an African Village Let Me Be in My Skin. Boston: Shambhala, 1999.

Jenkins, Mark. To Timbuktu: A Journey Down the Niger. New York: William Morrow and Company, 1997.

Kapuscinski, Ryszard. The Shadow of the Sun: My African Life. London: Penguin Books, 1998.

Morris, Kelly J. The Bight of Benin: Short Fiction. Atacore Press, 2007.

Packer, George. The Village of Waiting. New York: Random House, 1984.

Robinson, Mimi. Adinkra! West African Symbols. San Francisco: Chronicle Books, 1998.

Robinson, Mimi. Still It Makes Me Laugh: Impressions of West Africa. San Francisco: Chronicle Books, 1997.

Sandham, Fran. Traversa: A solo walk across Africa from the Skeleton Coast to the Indian Ocean. London: Duckworth Overlook, 2007.

Scott, Robyn. Twenty Chickens for a Saddle: The Story of an African Childhood. New York: The Penguin Press, 2008.

Shaffer, Tanya. Somebody's Heart is Burning: A Woman Wandered in Africa. New York: Vintage Books, 2003.

Smith, Julian. Crossing the Heart of Africa: An Odyssey of Love and Adventure. New York: Harper, 2010.

Spindel, Carol. In the Shadow of the Sacred Grove. New York, Random House, 1998.

Theroux, Paul. Dark Star Safari: Overland from Cairo to Cape Town. Boston, New York: Houghton Mifflin, 2003.

Thomas, Maria. African Visas: A Novella and Stories. New York: Soho Press, 1991.

Toffa, Francis. "The Togolese Family." Peace Corps Training Materials, 1971.

ABOUT THE AUTHOR

Meredith Pike-Baky is a writing teacher, gardener and grandmother. She has taught in the U.S. and internationally for many years and is currently co-facilitating a writing retreat in Girona, Spain. Among books she has coauthored are *Rain, Steam & Speed: Building Adolescent Fluency*, *Prompted to Write: Building On-Demand Writing Skills*, *Mosaic I and Mosaic II: Writing*, and *Tapestry: Writing 1 and 2*. She was a Peace Corps volunteer in Togo, West Africa in the 70's and returned to the Peace Corps three decades later as an Education Technical Trainer in Rwanda. She lives in northern California. Contact her at meredithpikebaky.com or at mpikebaky@mac.com.

Made in the USA
Las Vegas, NV
23 February 2021

18472576R00164